BASICS OF INSURANCE

Dr. M. Sirajudeen
Dr. T. Muthukumar
Dr. D. Sugumar

TANEESHA PUBLISHERS

Title : Basics of Insurance
Author : Dr. M. Sirajudeen, Dr. T. Muthukumar, Dr. D. Sugumar
Edition : First (March, 2025)
ISBN : 9789348037251

Published by

TANEESHA PUBLISHERS | *A Venture by -* **PRACHI DIGITAL PUBLICATION**

Regd. Add.: 254, Khuriyakhatta No. 10, Bindukhatta,
Lalkuan, Nainital - 262402, Uttarakhand, India
Website : www.taneeshapublishers.in
E-mail : taneeshapublishers@gmail.com
Phone : +91 8454 812712, +91 8057 812712

Printed by :
Manipal Technologies Limited, Bengaluru - 560001, Karnataka

Preface

This book offers a comprehensive exploration of the insurance landscape, designed to provide readers with a solid understanding of its fundamental principles, legal framework, and diverse applications. From the basic concepts of insurance to the intricacies of various policy types, this text aims to be a valuable resource for students, professionals, and anyone seeking to navigate the world of risk management. The book is structured to guide the reader through a logical progression of topics. It begins by laying the groundwork with an introduction to the core concepts of insurance, including its meaning, definition, features, functions, and principles. It also traces the historical evolution of insurance and examines its importance in modern society, along with an overview of the Indian insurance organization and recent sector developments. Building upon this foundation, the book delves into the legal dimensions that govern the insurance industry. It explores key legislation such as the LIC Act of 1956, the IRDA Act of 1999, and the General Insurance Act of 1972, providing insights into the regulatory framework that shapes the sector. A crucial aspect of the insurance ecosystem is the role of the agent. This book dedicates a chapter to understanding the intricacies of becoming an insurance agent, outlining the procedures, prerequisites, licensing requirements, functions, remuneration structures, and ethical considerations involved.The book then transitions into a detailed examination of various insurance products. It covers life insurance extensively, exploring its meaning, features, principles, functions, merits, demerits, types, and claims processes. Furthermore, it introduces other vital forms of insurance, including fire and health insurance. Finally, the book broadens its scope to encompass specialized insurance domains such as marine, motor, rural, crop, natural calamity, and theft insurance. This chapter provides an overview of the unique characteristics, principles, and procedures associated with each of these specialized areas.

Contents

Chapter – 1

Introduction

Insurance is a means of protection from financial loss. It is a form of risk management, primarily used to hedge against the risk of a contingent or uncertain loss. An entity which provides insurance is known as an insurer, insurance company, insurance carrier or underwriter. A person or entity who buys insurance is known as an insured or as a policyholder. The insurance transaction involves the insured assuming a guaranteed and known relatively small loss in the form of payment to the insurer in exchange for the insurer's promise to compensate the insured in the event of a covered loss. The loss may or may not be financial, but it must be reducible to financial terms, and usually involves something in w hich the insured has an insurable interest established by ownership, possession, or pre-existing relationship.

Meaning

An arrangement by which a company or the state undertakes to provide a guarantee of compensation for specified loss, damage, illness, or death in return for payment of a specified premium.

Definition

Insurance refers to a contractual arrangement in which one party, i.e. insurance company or the insurer agrees to compensate the loss or damage sustained to another party, i.e. the insured, by paying a definite amount, in exchange for an adequate consideration called as premium. It is often represented by an insurance policy, wherein the insured gets financial protection from the insurer against losses due to the occurrence of any event which is not under the control of the insured.

Types of Insurance

Basically, there are two types of insurance, as presented below

1.2. 1. Life Insurance

The insurance that covers the risk of the life of the insured is called Life insurance. In this, the nominee will get the policy amount, upon the death of the insurer. This is also called as an Assurance, as the event, i.e. death of the insured is certain. The payment of the policy amount on the maturity will be made in one shot (lump sum) or periodical instalments, i.e. annuity.

Whole life Assurance

Whole life assurance, is one in which the policy amount becomes due for payment on the death of the insured.

Term Life Assurance

The insurance policy in which the amount has to be paid on the maturity of the specified term, for instance, 10 years or 15 years, then it is called as term insurance policy.

Annuity

When the policy gets matured, the amount is paid in regular

installments, rather than in lump sum.

1.2. 2. General Insurance

Any insurance apart from life insurance comes under general insurance. In this type of insurance, the policyholder gets the compensation only when the loss is caused to him, due to the reasons indicated in the policy. It is also called as non-life insurance. It is classified into three categories:

1.2.3 Fire Insurance

A contractual arrangement in which the insurer promises to indemnify the loss caused to the goods and property of the insured due to fire, up to an agreed amount.

1.2.4 Marine Insurance

When in an insurance contract, the insurer undertakes to compensate the ship or cargo owner against the risks associated with the marine adventure, it is called as marine insurance. It is further divided into cargo insurance, hull insurance and freight insurance.

1.2.5 Miscellaneous Insurance

Apart from those discussed above, there are other types of general insurance business which cover different types of risks. It includes burglary insurance, credit insurance. Motor vehicle insurance, loss of profit insurance, fidelity insurance etc.

1.3 Features of Insurance

Insurance is a vital financial tool that provides protection against various risks. Here's a breakdown of its key features:

Core Features:

Risk Transfer:

The fundamental principle of insurance is to transfer risk from an individual or entity (the insured) to an insurance company (the insurer).

Premium Payment:

The insured pays a regular fee, known as a premium, to the insurer in exchange for this risk transfer.

Sum Assured/Sum Insured:

This is the amount of money the insurer agrees to pay in the event of a covered loss.

"Sum assured" is often used in life insurance, while "sum insured" is more common in other types of insurance.

Policy Term:

Insurance policies are valid for a specific period, known as the policy term.

Claim Settlement:

When a covered loss occurs, the insured files a claim with the insurer. The insurer then assesses the claim and, if valid, pays out the agreed-upon amount.

Contractual Agreement:

Insurance is a legally binding contract between the insurer and the insured.

Principle of Utmost Good Faith:

Both parties are expected to be honest and transparent in their dealings.

Additional Features:

Tax Benefits:

Many insurance policies offer tax advantages, such as deductions on premiums paid.

Riders and Add-ons:

These are optional features that can be added to a policy to provide extra coverage.

No-Claim Bonus (NCB):

In some types of insurance, such as motor and health insurance, policyholders may receive a discount on their renewal premium if they don't file any claims.

Digitalization:

Many insurance companies now provide online services, making it easier to purchase policies, pay premiums, and file claims.

Concepts:

Deductible: The amount the insured must pay out of pocket before the insurer begins to cover costs.

Policy Limit: The maximum amount the insurer will pay for a covered loss.

1.4 Functions of Insurance

The functions of insurance can be studied into two parts (i) Primary Functions, and (ii) Secondary Functions as discussed below.

(i) Primary Functions

To provide protection against the probable chances of loss

The time and amount of loss are uncertain and at the happening of risk, the person will suffer loss in absence of insurance. The insurance guarantees the payment of loss and thus protects the assured from sufferings.

Risk-Sharing

The risk is uncertain, and therefore, the loss arising from the risk is also uncertain. When risk takes place, the loss is shared by all the persons who are exposed to the risk. The risk-sharing in ancient time was done only at time of damage or death; but today, on the basis of probability of risk, the share is obtained from each and every insured in the shape of premium without which protection is not guaranteed by the insurer.

Secondary functions

Prevention of Loss

The insurance joins hands with those institutions which are engaged in preventing the losses of the society because the reduction in loss causes lesser payment to the assured and so more saving is possible which will assist in reducing the premium. Lesser premium invites more business and more business cause lesser share to the assured.

It Provides Capital:

The insurance provides capital to the society. The accumulated funds are invested in productive channel. The dearth of capital of the society is minimized to a greater extent with the help of investment of insurance. The industry, the business and the individual are benefited by the investment and loans of the insurers.

It Improves Efficiency:

The insurance eliminates worries and miseries of losses at death and destruction of property. The carefree person can devote his body and soul together for better achievement. It improves not only his efficiency, but the efficiencies of the masses are also advanced.

It helps Economic Progress

The insurance by protecting the society from huge losses of damage, destruction and death, provides an initiative to work hard for the betterment of the masses. The next factor of economic progress, the capital, is also immensely provided by the masses. The property, the valuable assets, the man, the machine and the society cannot lose much at the disaster.

1.5 Principles of Insurance

Principle of Utmost Good Faith (Uberrimae Fidei):

Both the insurer and the insured must disclose all material facts accurately and honestly. This principle emphasizes trust and transparency.

Principle of Insurable Interest:

The insured must have a financial interest in the subject matter of the insurance. This means they would suffer a financial loss if the insured event occurred. This principle prevents gambling on losses.

Principle of Indemnity:

The insurer aims to restore the insured to their financial position before the loss occurred. This principle prevents the insured from profiting from a loss. This principle is most applicable to property insurance.

Principle of Contribution:

If the insured has multiple insurance policies covering the same risk, each insurer will contribute proportionally to the loss. This prevents the insured from collecting more than the actual loss.

Principle of Subrogation:

After paying a claim, the insurer has the right to pursue any third party responsible for the loss. This allows the insurer to recover the amount paid to the insured.

Principle of Proximate Cause (Causa Proxima):

The insurer is only liable for losses directly caused by an insured peril. The proximate cause is the dominant cause of the loss.

Principle of Loss Minimization:

The insured has a duty to take reasonable steps to minimize the loss after an insured event occurs.

1.6 Evolution of insurance

India had the nineteenth largest insurance market in the world in 2003. Strong economic growth in the last decade combined with a population of over one billion makes it one of the potentially largest markets in the future. Insurance in India has gone through two radical transformations. Before 1956, Insurance was private with minimal government intervention. In 1956, life insurance was nationalized and a monopoly was created. In 1972, general insurance was nationalized as well.255 But, unlike life insurance, a different structure was created for the industry. One holding company was formed with four subsidiaries. As a part of the general opening up of the economy after 1992, a government-appointed committee recommended that private companies should be allowed to operate. It took six years to implement the recommendation. The private sector was allowed into the insurance business in 2000. However, foreign ownership was restricted. No more than 26 percent of any company can be foreign-owned

1.7 Milestones of Insurance Regulations

1912 The Indian Life Insurance Company Act

1938 The Insurance Act: Comprehensive Act to regulate insurance business in India

1956 Nationalization of life insurance business in India

1972 Nationalization of general insurance business in India

1993 Setting up of Malhotra Committee

1994 Recommendations of Malhotra Committee

1995 Setting up of Mukherjee Committee

1996 Setting up of (interim) Insurance Regulatory Authority (IRA)

1997 Mukherjee Committee Report submitted but not made public

1997 The Government gives greater autonomy to LIC, GIC and its subsidiaries with regard to the restructuring of boards and flexibility in investment norms aimed at channeling funds to the infrastructure sector

1998 The cabinet decides to allow 40% foreign equity in private insurance companies-26% to foreign companies and 14% to NRI's, OCB's and FII's

1999. The Standing Committee headed by Murali Deora decides that foreign equity in private insurance should be limited to 26%. The IRA bill is renamed the Insurance Regulatory and Development Authority (IRDA) Bill.

1999 Cabinet clears IRDA Bill

2000 President Gives Assent to the IRDA Bill

1.8 Advantages and disadvantages of insurance

1.8.1 Advantages of insurance

The following are the advantages of insurance:

1. Providing Security:

There is always a fear of sudden loss. There may be a fire in the factory, storm in the sea or loss of a life. In all these cases it becomes difficult to bear the loss. Insurance provides a cover against any sudden loss. In case of marine and fire insurance the loss suffered by the insured is fully compensated and he is restored to his earlier position.

In the same way, if a bread-bringing member of the family dies prematurely, the family is provided with money to continue with its livelihood. So, insurance gives security to both individual and business-man. These days insurance covers various social welfare schemes also. There are schemes providing for unemployment, sickness, accident, health and old age insurances. These schemes are helpful for poor people and help in establishing social justice.

2. Spreading of Risk:

The basic principle of insurance is to spread risk among a large number of people. A large number of persons get insurance policies and pay premium to the insurer. Whenever a loss occurs, it is compensated out of funds of the insurer. The loss is spread among a large number of policy-holders.

Insurance covers the loss of an individual but the social loss cannot be eliminated. If the property of a person is lost by fire, he will be compensated by the insurance company. The loss of goods will remain as a social loss. Insurance cannot eliminate loss but it can reduce the risk to the individual.

3. Source for Collecting Funds:

In lieu of an insurance cover, the insured pays premium to the insurer. The premium is received regularly in installments. Large funds are collected by way of premium. These funds can be gainfully employed in industrial development of a country. Life insurance policies are purchased by persons from all walks of life. It helps in collecting savings from a large number of persons.

In India, Life Insurance Corporation of India provides large funds to the industries for long-term investments. These funds are productively used in exploiting natural resources which accelerates industrial growth of a country. The employment opportunities are also increased by big investments made by insurance companies. So, insurance has become an important source of capital formation.

4. Encourage Savings:

Insurance does not only protect risks but it provides an investment channel too. Life insurance provides a mode of investment. The insurance develops a habit of saving money by paying premium. The amount of policy is paid to the insured or to his nominees. In case of fixed time policies, the insured gets a lump-sum amount after the maturity of the policy.

5. Encourage International Trade:

International trade involves many risks in transporting goods from one country to another. In the absence of insurance the traders will always be worried for the safe arrival of goods. The quantum of trade will be limited because of uncertainties and risk involved during transit. Insurance provides protection against all types of sea-risks. It has helped the development of international trade on a large scale.

In lieu of an insurance cover, the insured pays premium to the insurer. The premium is received regularly in installments. Large funds are collected by way of premium. These funds can be gainfully employed in industrial development of a country. Life insurance policies are purchased by persons from all walks of life. It helps in collecting savings from a large number of persons.

In India, Life Insurance Corporation of India provides large funds to the industries for long-term investments. These funds are productively used in exploiting natural resources which accelerates industrial growth of a country. The employment opportunities are also increased by big investments made by insurance companies. So, insurance has become an important source of capital formation.

4. Encourage Savings:

Insurance does not only protect risks but it provides an investment channel too. Life insurance provides a mode of investment. The insurance develops a habit of saving money by paying premium. The amount of policy is paid to the insured or to his nominees. In case of fixed time policies, the insured gets a lump-sum amount after the maturity of the policy.

5. Encourage International Trade:

International trade involves many risks in transporting goods from one country to another. In the absence of insurance the traders will always be worried for the safe arrival of goods. The quantum of trade will be limited because of uncertainties and risk involved during transit. Insurance provides protection against all types of sea-risks. It has helped the development of international trade on a large scale.

1.8.2 Disadvantages of Insurance

1. Can be expensive

A major fear of insurance buyers is the price they have to pay. Sometimes, depending on the policy and certain factors that affect the cost, such as credit score and other potential risks to the insurance company, buying insurance can be expensive.

But if bought at a right time, with the right reason and right amount of coverage, you might actually get the right price.

2. Rising premiums

Most types of insurances have varying rates of premiums, and you should be very careful about it. Before buying a policy, make sure you know from the beginning if you have a guaranteed premium throughout the policy, or if it changes from time to time in relation to inflation. You should weigh out if you prefer a fixed premium or you'€™d like to take the risk, and more importantly, determine the amount you can afford to spare on the contract.

3. Claims might not be paid out

Sometimes this issue also becomes a public misconception which drives insurance buyers away. While it'€™s true that there are cases of denied claims, there's a ground for this to happen and thus shouldn't scare you away. For one, you might have presented wrong information during the underlying process. Or you weren't able to satisfy some requirements, or performed certain actions that could lead to nullification of your contract. To avoid this from happening, you need to be honest from the very beginning with your provider, and clarify any limitations or exclusions that could lead to denied claims.

1.9 Importance of Insurance

All assets have some economic value attached to them. There is also a possibility that these assets may get damaged/destroyed or become non-operational due to risks like breakdowns, fire, floods, earthquake etc. Different assets are exposed to different types of risks like a car has a risk of theft or meeting an accident, a house is exposed to risk of catching fire, a human is exposed to risk of death/accident. Hence insurance is required for the following reasons:

Insurance acts as an important tool in providing a sense of security to the society on a whole. In case the bread earner of a family dies, the family suffers from direct financial loss as family's income ceases. Life insurance is one alternate arrangement that offers some respite to the family from financial distress.

The basic need of insurance arises as risks are uncertain and unpredictable in nature. Getting insurance for an asset does not mean that the asset is protected against risks or its exposure to risk is reduced, but it actually implies that in case the asset suffers any loss in value due to such risk, the insurance company bears the loss and compensates the insured by making payment to him.

Insurance acts as a useful instrument in promoting savings and investments, particularly within the lower income and middle income families. These savings are used as investments to fuel economic growth.

1.10 Insurance organization in India

Insurance organization in India

The Present of Insurance Sector In India

So far as the industry goes, LIC, New India, National Insurance, United insurance and Oriental are the only government ruled entity that stands high both in the market share as well as their contribution to the Insurance sector in India. There are two specialized insurers – Agriculture Insurance Company Ltd catering to Crop Insurance and Export Credit Guarantee of India catering to Credit Insurance. Whereas, others are the private insurers (both life and general) who have done a joint venture with foreign insurance companies to start their insurance businesses in India

1.10.1 Life Insurance Companies:

Private Sector Companies

Aegon Life Insurance Co. Ltd.

Aviva Life Insurance Co. India Ltd.

Bajaj Allianz Life Insurance Co. Ltd.

Bharti AXA Life Insurance Co. Ltd.

Birla Sun Life Insurance Co. Ltd.

Canara HSBC Oriental Bank of Commerce Life Insurance Co. Ltd.

DHFL Pramerica Life Insurance Co. Ltd.

Edelweiss Tokio Life Insurance Co. Ltd

Exide Life Insurance Co. Ltd.

Future Generali India Life Insurance Co. Ltd.

HDFC Standard Life Insurance Co. Ltd.

ICICI Prudential Life Insurance Co. Ltd.
IDBI Federal Life Insurance Co. Ltd.
IndiaFirst Life Insurance Co. Ltd
Kotak Mahindra Old Mutual Life Insurance Ltd.
Max Life Insurance Co. Ltd.
PNB MetLife India Insurance Co. Ltd.
Reliance Life Insurance Co. Ltd.
Sahara India Life Insurance Co. Ltd.
SBI Life Insurance Co. Ltd.
Shriram Life Insurance Co. Ltd.
Star Union Dai-Ichi Life Insurance Co. Ltd.
Tata AIA Life Insurance Co. Ltd.

1.10.2 General Insurancc Companies:

Private Sector Companies

Aditya Birla Health Insurance Co. Ltd.
Bajaj Allianz General Insurance Co. Ltd.
Bharti AXA General Insurance Co.Ltd.
Cholamandalam General Insurance Co. Ltd.
Future Generali India Insurance Co.Ltd.
HDFC ERGO General Insurance Co. Ltd.
ICICI Lombard General Insurance Co. Ltd.
IFFCO-Tokio General Insurance Co. Ltd.
Kotak General Insurance Co. Ltd.
L&T General Insurance Co. Ltd.
Liberty Videocon General Insurance Co. Ltd.
Magma HDI General Insurance Co. Ltd.
Raheja QBE General Insurance Co. Ltd.
Reliance General Insurance Co. Ltd.
Royal Sundaram Alliance Insurance Co. Ltd
SBI General Insurance Co. Ltd.
Shriram General Insurance Co. Ltd.
TATA AIG General Insurance Co. Ltd.
Universal Sompo General Insurance Co.Ltd.
Health Insurance Companies

Apollo Munich Health Insurance Co.Ltd.

Star Health Allied Insurance Co. Ltd.

Max Bupa Health Insurance Co. Ltd.

Religare Health Insurance Co. Ltd.

Cigna TTK Health Insurance Co. Ltd.

This collaboration with the foreign markets has made the Insurance Sector in India only grow tremendously with a high current market share. India allowed private companies in insurance sector in 2000, setting a limit on FDI to 26%, which was increased to 49% in 2014. IRDAI states – Insurance Laws (Amendment) Act, 2015 provides for enhancement of the Foreign Investment Cap in an Indian Insurance Company from 26% to an Explicitly Composite Limit of 49% with the safeguard of Indian Ownership and Control. Private insurers like HDFC, ICICI and SBI have been some tough competitors for providing life as well as non-life products to the insurance sector in India.

1.11 The Future of Insurance Sector in India

Though LIC continues to dominate the Insurance sector in India, the introduction of the new private insurers will see a vibrant expansion and growth of both life and non-life sectors in 2017. The demands for new insurance policies with pocket-friendly premiums are sky high. Since the domestic economy cannot grow drastically, the insurance sector in India is controlled for a strong growth.

With the increase in income and exponential growth of purchasing power as well as household savings, the insurance sector in India would introduce emerging trends like product innovation, multi-distribution, better claims management and regulatory trends in the Indian market.

The government also strives hard to provide insurance to individuals in a below poverty line by introducing schemes like the

- Pradhan Mantri Suraksha Bima Yojana (PMSBY),
- Rashtriya Swasthya Bima Yojana (RSBY) and
- Pradhan Mantri Jeevan Jyoti Bima Yojana (PMJJBY).

Introduction of these schemes would help the lower and lower-middle income categories to utilize the new policies with lower premiums in India.

With several regulatory changes in the insurance sector in India, the future looks pretty awesome and promising for the life insurance industry. This would further lead to a change in the way insurers take care of the business and engage proactively with its genuine buyers. Some demographic factors like the growing insurance awareness of the insurance, retirement planning, growing middle class and young insurable crowd will substantially increase the growth of the Insurance sector in India.

1.12 Investments and Recent Developments

The insurance sector is undergoing significant changes, driven by technological advancements, evolving customer expectations, and regulatory shifts. Here's a look at investments and recent developments in insurance:

Investments in Insurance:

Technological Investments (Insurtech):

A major trend is the influx of investments into Insurtech companies. These companies are using technology like AI, machine learning, and data analytics to streamline processes, improve customer experiences, and create innovative insurance products

Investments are focused on areas like

- Digital distribution and customer engagement.
- Automated claims processing.
- Data-driven underwriting.
- Personalized insurance products.

Private Equity Investments:

Private equity firms are increasingly investing in insurance distribution, especially in commercial lines. This is driven by factors like the complexity of risks and the potential for consolidation.

Insurance companies themselves are also diversifying their investment portfolios, seeking higher yields through various asset classes.

Focus on Sustainable Investments (ESG):

There's a growing emphasis on incorporating environmental,

social, and governance (ESG) factors into insurance investment strategies. This reflects increasing awareness of climate change and social responsibility.

Recent Developments in Insurance

Digital Transformation:

The insurance industry is rapidly digitizing its operations, from online policy purchases to mobile claims filing.

This includes increased use of:

- Artificial intelligence (AI) and machine learning.
- Data analytics.
- Cloud computing.

Personalized Insurance Products:

Insurers are leveraging data to create personalized insurance products that cater to individual customer needs.This includes usage-based insurance (UBI) for auto insurance and personalized health insurance plans.

Increased Regulatory Scrutiny:

Regulatory bodies are increasingly focusing on areas like data privacy, cybersecurity, and financial stability. There are also changes to regulations regarding foreign direct investment (FDI) in many countries, including India, which affect the insurance sector.

Focus on Microinsurance:

There is a growing focus on microinsurance, which is designed to provide affordable insurance coverage to low-income individuals and communities.

Composite Licensing:

In some regions there is a movement to allow composite licensing, so that Insurers can offer both life and non-life insurance products. This is intended to increase customer options, and reduce costs.

Increased awareness of climate risk:

Insurers are having to adapt to the increasing risks of climate change, this is affecting how they calculate risk, and what products they offer.

1.13 Government Initatives

- The Government of India has taken a number of initiatives to boost the insurance industry. Some of them are as follows:
- As per Union Budget 2019-20, 100 per cent foreign direct investment (FDI) permitted for insurance intermediaries.
- In September 2018, National Health Protection Scheme was launched under Ayushman Bharat to provide coverage of up to Rs 500,000 (US$ 7,723) to more than 100 million vulnerable families. The scheme is expected to increase penetration of health insurance in India from 34 per cent to 50 per cent.
- Over 47.9 million famers were benefitted under Pradhan Mantri Fasal Bima Yojana (PMFBY) in 2017-18.
- The Insurance Regulatory and Development Authority of India (IRDAI) plans to issue redesigned initial public offering (IPO) guidelines for insurance companies in India, which are to looking to divest equity through the IPO route.
- IRDAI has allowed insurers to invest up to 10 per cent in additional tier 1 (AT1) bonds that are issued by banks to augment their tier 1 capital, in order to expand the pool of eligible investors for the banks.

Chapter – 2

LIC Act 1956

Introduction

Life Insurance Business in India was nationalized with effect from January 19, 1956. On the date, the Indian business of 16 non-Indian insurers operating in India and 75 Provident Societies were taken over by Government of India. Life Insurance Corporation of India, Act was passed by the Parliament on June 18, 1956 and came into effect from July 1, 1956. Life Insurance Corporation of India commenced its functioning as a corporate body from September 1, 1956. Its working is governed by the LIC Act. The LIC is a corporate having perpetual succession and a common seal with a power to acquire hold and dispose of property and can by its name sue and be sued.

2.1 Important Provisions of LIC Act 1956

- Constitution
- Capital
- Functions of the Corporation
- Transfer of Services
- Set-up of the Corporation
- Committee of the Corporation
- Authorities
- Finance, Accounts and Audit
- Miscellaneous

2.2 Overview of LIC

The LIC of India was set up under the LIC Act, 1956 under which the life insurance was nationalized. As a result, business of 243 insurance companies was taken over by LIC on 1-9- 1956.

It is basically an investment institution, in as much as the funds of policy holders are invested and dispersed over different classes of securities, industries and regions, to safeguard their maximum interest on long term basis. LIC is required to invest not less than 75% of its funds in Central and State Government securities, the government guaranteed marketable securities and in the socially-oriented sectors. At present, it is the largest institutional investor. It provides long term finance to industries. Besides, it extends resource support to other term lending institutions by way of subscription to their shares and bonds and also by way of term loans. LIC which has entered into its 57th year has emerged as the world's largest insurance co. in terms of number of policies covered. The LIC's total coverage of policies including individual, group and social schemes has crossed the 11 crore.

2.3 Objectives of LIC of India

The LIC was established with the following objectives

- Spread life insurance widely and in particular to the rural areas, to the socially and economically backward claries with a view to reaching all insurable persons in the country and providing them adequate financial cover against death at a reasonable cost Maximisation of mobilisation of people's savings for nation building activities.
- Provide complete security and promote efficient service to the policy-holders at economic premium rates.
- Conduct business with utmost economy and with the full realisation that the money belong to the policy holders.
- Act as trustees of the insured public in their individual and collective capacities.
- Meet the various life insurance needs of the community that would arise in the changing social and economic environment
- Involve all people working in the corporation to the best of their capability in furthering the interest of the insured public by providing efficient service with courtesy.

2.4 Role and Functions of LIC

- It collects the savings of the people through life policies and invests the fund in a variety of investments.
- It invests the funds in profitable investments so as to get good return. Hence the policy holders get benefits in the form of lower rates of premium and increased bonus. In short, LIC is

answerable to the policy holders.

- It subscribes to the shares of companies and corporations. It is a major shareholder in a large number of blue chip companies.
- It provides direct loans to industries at a lower rate of interest. It is giving loans to industrial enterprises to the extent of 12% of its total commitment.
- It provides refinancing activities through SFCs in different states and other industrial loangiving institutions.
- It has provided indirect support to industry through subscriptions to shares and bonds of financial institutions such as IDBI, IFCI, ICICI, SFCs etc. at the time when they required initial capital. It also directly subscribed to the shares of Agricultural Refinance Corporation and SBI.
- It gives loans to those projects which are important for national economic welfare. The socially oriented projects such as electrification, sewage and water channelising are given priority by the LIC.
- It nominates directors on the boards of companies in which it makes its investments.
- It gives housing loans at reasonable rates of interest.
- It acts as a link between the saving and the investing process. It generates the savings of the small savers, middle income group and the rich through several schemes.
- Normerly LIC has played a major role in the Indian capital market. To stabilize the capital market it has underwritten capital issues. But recently it has moved to other avenues of financing. Now it has become very selective in its underwriting pattern

2.5 Insurance Regulatory and Development Authority Act, 1999

To provide for the establishment of an Authority to protect the interests of holders of insurance policies, to regulate, promote and ensure orderly growth of the insurance industry and for matters connected therewith or incidental thereto and further to amdend the

Insurance Act, 1938, the Life Insurance Corporation Act, 1956 and the General Insurance Business(Nationalization) Act, 1972.

2.6 CHAPTER I

Preliminary

1. Short title, extent and commencement.-

(1)This Act may be called the Insurance Regulatory and Development Authority Act, 1999.

(2) It extends to the whole of India.

(3) It shall come into force on such date as the Central Government may, by notification in the Official Gazette, appoint:

Provided that different dates may be appointed for different provisions of this Act and any reference in any such provision to the commencement of this Act shall be construed as a reference to the coming into force of that provision.

2. Definitions

(1) In this Act, unless the context otherwise requires, -

(a) "Appointed day" means the date on which the Authority is established under sub-section (1) of section 3;

(b) "Authority" means the Insurance Regulatory and Development Authority established under sub-section (1) of section 3;

(c) "Chairperson" means the Chairperson of the Authority;

(d) "Fund" means the Insurance Regulatory and Development Authority Fund constituted under sub-section (1) of section 16;

(e) "Interim Insurance Regulatory Authority" means the Insurance Regulatory Authority set up by the Central Government through Resolution No.17(2)/94-Ins-V, dated the 23rd January, 1996;

(f) "intermediary or insurance intermediary" includes insurance brokers, reinsurance brokers, insurance consultants, surveyors and loss assessors;

(g) "member" means a whole time or a part time member of the Authority and includes the Chairperson;

(h) "notification" means a notification published in the Official Gazette;

(i) "prescribed" means prescribed by rules made under this Act;

(j) "regulations" means the regulations made by the Authority.

(2) Words and expressions used and not defined in this Act but defined in the Insurance Act, 1938 (4 of 1938) or the Life Insurance Corporation Act, 1956 (31 of 1956) or the General Insurance Business (Nationalisation) Act, 1972 (57 of 1972) shall have the meanings respectively assigned to them in those Acts.

2.7 Chapter II

Insurance Regulatory and Development Authority

3. Establishment and incorporation of authority

(1) With effect from such date as the Central Government may, by notification, appoint, there shall be established, for the purposes of this Act, an Authority to be called "the Insurance Regulatory and Development Authority".

(2) The Authority shall be a body corporate by the name aforesaid having perpetual succession and a common seal with power, subject to the provisions of this Act, to acquire, hold and dispose of property, both movable and immovable, and to contract and shall, by the said name, sue or be sued.

(3) The head office of the Authority shall be at such place as the Central Government may decide from time to time.

(4) The Authority may establish offices at other places in India.

4. Composition of Authority.

The Authority shall consist of the following members, namely:-

(a) A Chairperson;

(b) Not more than five whole-time members;

(c) Not more than four part-time members,

to be appointed by the Central Government from amongst persons of ability, integrity and standing who have knowledge or experience in life insurance, general insurance, actuarial science, finance, economics, law, accountancy, administration or any other discipline which would, in the opinion of the Central Government, be useful to the Authority:

Provided that the Central Government shall, while appointing the Chairperson and the whole-time members, ensure that at least one person each is a person having knowledge or experience in life insurance, general insurance or actuarial science, respectively.

5. Tenure of office of chairperson and other members

(1) The Chairperson and every other whole-time member shall hold office for a term of five years from the date on which he enters upon his office and shall be eligible for reappointment:

Provided that no person shall hold office as a Chairperson after he has attained the age of sixty-five years:

Provided further that no person shall hold office as a whole-time member after he has attained the age of sixty-two years.

(2) A part-time member shall hold office for a term not exceeding five years from the date on which he enters upon his office.

(3) Notwithstanding anything contained in sub-section (1) or sub-section (2), a member may -

(a) relinquish his office by giving in writing to the Central Government notice of not less than three months; or

(b) be removed from his office in accordance with the provisions of section

6. Removal from Office

1) The Central Government may remove from office any member who-

(a) is, or at any time has been, adjudged as an insolvent; or

(b) Has become physically or mentally incapable of acting as a member; or

(c) has been convicted of any offence which, in the opinion of the Central Government, involves moral turpitude; or

(d) has acquired such financial or other interest as is likely to affect prejudicially his functions as a member; or

(e) has so abused his position as to render his continuation in office detrimental to the public interest.

(2) No such member shall be removed under clause (d) or clause (e) of sub-section (1) unless he has been given a reasonable opportunity of being heard in the matter.

7. Salary and allowances of chairperson and members

(1) The salary and allowances payable to, and other terms and conditions of service of, the members other than part-time members shall be such as may be prescribed.

(2) The part-time members shall receive such allowances as may be prescribed.

(3) The salary, allowances and other conditions of service of a member shall not be varied to his disadvantage after appointment.

8. Bar on future employment of members.

The Chairperson and the whole-time members shall not, for a period of two years from the date on which they cease to hold office as such, except with the previous approval of the Central Government, accept-

(a) any employment either under the Central Government or under any State Government; or

(b) any appointment in any company in the insurance sector.

9. Administrative powers of chairperson.

The Chairperson shall have the powers of general superintendence and direction in respect of all administrative matters of the Authority.

10. Meetings of authority

(1) The Authority shall meet at such times and places and shall observe such rules and procedures in regard to transaction of business at its meetings (including quorum at such meetings) as may be determined by the regulations.

(2) The Chairperson, or if for any reason he is unable to attend a meeting of the Authority, any other member chosen by the members present from amongst themselves at the meeting shall preside at the meeting.

(3) All questions which come up before any meeting of the Authority shall be decided by a majority of votes by the members present and voting, and in the event of an equality of votes, the Chairperson, or in his absence, the person presiding shall have a second or casting vote.

(4) The Authority may make regulations for the transaction of business at its meetings.

11. vacancies, etc., not to invalidate proceedings of authority

No act or proceeding of the Authority shall be invalid merely by reason of -

(a) any vacancy in, or any defect in the constitution of, the Authority; or

(b) any defect in the appointment of a person acting as a member of the Authority; or

(c) any irregularity in the procedure of the Authority not affecting the merits of the case.

12. Officers and employees of authority

(1) The Authority may appoint officers and such other employees as it considered necessary for the efficient discharge of its function under this Act.

(2) The terms and other conditions of service of officers and other employees of the Authority appointed under sub-section(1) shall be governed by regulations made under this Act.

2.8 Chapter III

Transfer of assets, liabilities, etc., of interim insurance regulatory authority

13. transfer of assets, liabilities, etc., of interim insurance regulatory authority

On the appointed day,-

(a) all the assets and liabilities of the Interim Insurance Regulatory Authority shall stand transferred to, and vested in, the Authority.

Explanation - The assets of the Interim Insurance Regulatory Authority shall be deemed to include all rights and powers, and all properties, whether movable or immovable, including, in particular, cash balances, deposits and all other interests and rights in, or arising out of, such properties as may be in the possession of the Interim Insurance Regulatory Authority and all books of account and other documents relating to the same; and liabilities shall be deemed to include all debts, liabilities and obligations of whatever kind;

(b) without prejudice to the previous of clause (a), all debts, obligations and liabilities incurred, all contracts entered into and all matters and things engaged to be done by, with or for the Interim Insurance Regulatory Authority immediately before that day, for or in connection with the purpose of the said Regulatory Authority, shall be deemed to have been incurred, entered into or engaged to be done by, with or for, the Authority;

(c) all sums of money due to the Interim Insurance Regulatory Authority immediately before that day shall be deemed to be due to the Authority; and

(d) all suits and other legal proceedings instituted or which could have been instituted by or against the Interim Insurance Regulatory Authority immediately before that day may be continued or may be instituted by or against the Authority.

2.9 Chapter IV

Duties, powers and functions of authority

14. Duties, powers and functions of authority

(1) Subject to the provisions of this Act and any other law for the time being in force, the Authority shall have the duty to regulate, promote and ensure orderly growth of the insurance business and re-insurance business.

(2) Without prejudice to the generality of the provisions contained in sub-section (1), the powers and functions of the Authority shall include, -

(a) Issue to the applicant a certificate of registration, renew, modify, withdraw, suspend or cancel such registration;

(b) protection of the interests of the policy holders in matters concerning assigning of policy, nomination by policy holders, insurable interest, settlement of insurance claim, surrender value of policy and other terms and conditions of contracts of insurance;

(c) specifying requisite qualifications, code of conduct and practical training for intermediary or insurance intermediaries and agents;

(d) specifying the code of conduct for surveyors and loss assessors;

(e) promoting efficiency in the conduct of insurance business;

(f) promoting and regulating professional organisations connected with the insurance and re-insurance business;

(g) Levying fees and other charges for carrying out the purposes of this Act;

(h) calling for information from, undertaking inspection of, conducting enquiries and investigations including audit of the insurers, intermediaries, insurance intermediaries and other organisations connected with the insurance business;

(i) control and regulation of the rates, advantages, terms and conditions that may be offered by insurers in respect of general insurance business not so controlled and regulated by the Tariff Advisory Committee under section 64U of the Insurance Act, 1938 (4 of 1938);

(j) specifying the form and manner in which books of account shall be maintained and statement of accounts shall be rendered by insurers and other insurance intermediaries;

(k) regulating investment of funds by insurance companies;

(l) regulating maintenance of margin of solvency;

(m) adjudication of disputes between insurers and intermediaries or insurance intermediaries;

(n) supervising the functioning of the Tariff Advisory Committee;

(o) specifying the percentage of premium income of the insurer to finance schemes for promoting and regulating professional organisations referred to in clause (f);

(p) specifying the percentage of life insurance business and general insurance business to be undertaken by the insurer in the rural or social sector; and

(q) exercising such other powers as may be prescribed.

2.10 Chapter V

Finance, accounts and audit

15. Grants by central government

The Central Government may, after due appropriation made by Parliament by law in this behalf, make to the Authority grants of such sums of money as the Government may think fit for being utilised for the purposes of this Act.

16. Constitution of funds

(1) There shall be constituted a fund to be called "the Insurance Regulatory and Development Authority Fund" and there shall be credited thereto-

(a) all Government grants, fees and charges received by the Authority;

(b) all sums received by the Authority from such other source as may be decided upon by the Central Government;

(c) the percentage of prescribed premium income received from the insurer.

(2) The Fund shall be applied for meeting -

(a) the salaries, allowances and other remuneration of the members, officers and other employees of the Authority;

(b) the other expenses of the Authority in connection with the discharge of its functions and for the purposes of this Act.

17. Accounts and audit

(1) The Authority shall maintain proper accounts and other relevant records and prepare an annual statement of accounts in such form as may be prescribed by the Central Government in consultation with the Comptroller and Auditor-General of India.

(2) The accounts of the Authority shall be audited by the Comptroller and Auditor-General of India at such intervals as may be specified by him and any expenditure incurred in connection with such audit shall be payable by the Authority to the Comptroller and Auditor-General.

(3) The Comptroller and Auditor-General of India and any other person appointed by him in connection with the audit of the accounts of the Authority shall have the same rights, privileges and authority in connection with such audit as the Comptroller and Auditor-General generally has in connection with the audit of the Government accounts and, in particular, shall have the right to demand the production of books of account, connected vouchers and other documents and papers and to inspect any of the offices of the Authority.

(4) The accounts of the Authority as certified by the Comptroller and Auditor-General of India or any other person appointed by him in this behalf together with the audit-report thereon shall be forwarded annually to the Central Government and that Government shall cause the same to be laid before each House of Parliament.

2.11 Chapter VI

Miscellaneous

18. Power of central government to issue directions

(1) Without prejudice to the foregoing provisions of this Act, the Authority shall, in exercise of its powers or the performance of its functions under this Act, be bound by such directions on questions of policy, other than those relating to technical and administrative matters, as the Central Government may give in writing to it from time to time. Provided that the Authority shall, as far as practicable, be given an opportunity to express its views before any direction is given under this sub-section.

(2)The decision of the Central Government, whether a question is one of policy or not, shall be final.

19. Power of central government to supersede authority

(1) If at any time the Central Government is of the opinion-

(a)that, on account of circumstances beyond the control of the Authority, it is unable to discharge the functions or perform the duties imposed on it by or under the provisions of this Act, or

(b) that the Authority has persistently defaulted in complying with any direction given by the Central Government under this Act or in the discharge of the functions or performance of the duties imposed on it by or under the provisions of this Act and as a result of such default the financial position of the Authority or the administration of the Authority has suffered; or

(c) that circumstances exist which render it necessary in the public interest so to do, the Central Government may, be notification and for reasons to be specified therein, supersede the Authority for such period, not exceeding six months, as may be specified in the notification and appoint a person to be the Controller of Insurance under section 2B of the Insurance Act, 1938 (4 of 1938), if not already done Provided that before issuing any such notification, the Central Government shall give a reasonable opportunity to the Authority to make representations, if any, of the Authority.

(2) Upon the publication of a notification under sub-section(1) superseding the Authority, -

(a) The Chairperson and other members shall, as from the date of supersession, vacate their offices as such;

(b) all the powers, functions and duties which may, by or under the provisions of this Act, be exercised or discharged by or on behalf of the Authority shall, until the Authority is reconstituted under sub-section(3), be exercised and discharged by the Controller of Insurance; and

(c)all properties owned or controlled by the Authority shall, until the Authority is reconstituted under sub-section

(3) Vest in the Central Government.

(3)On or before the expiration of the period of supersession specified in the notification issued under sub-section (1), the Central Government shall reconstitute the Authority by a fresh appointment of its Chairperson and other members and in such case any person who had vacated his office under clause(a) of sub-section(2) shall not be deemed to be disqualified for reappointment.

(4) The Central Government shall cause a copy of the notification issued under sub-section(1) and a full report to any action to be laid before each House of Parliament at the earliest.

20. furnishing of returns, etc., to central government

(1) The Authority shall furnish to the Central Government at such time and in such form and manner as may be prescribed, or as the Central Government may direct to furnish such returns, statements and other particulars in regard to any proposed or existing programme for the promotion and development of the insurance industry as the Central Government may, from time to time, require.

(2) Without prejudice to the provisions of sub-section(1), the Authority shall, within nine months after the close of each financial year, submit to the Central Government a report giving a true and full account of its activities including the activities for promotion and development of the insurance business during the previous financial year.

(3) Copies of the reports received under sub-section(2) shall be laid, as soon as may be after they are received, before each House of Parliament.

21. chairperson, members, officers and other employees of authority to be public servants

The Chairperson, members, officers and other employees of Authority shall be deemed, when acting or purporting to act in pursuance of any of the provisions of this Act, to be public servants within the meaning of section 21 of the Indian Penal Code (45 of 1860).

22. protection of action taken in good faith

No suit, prosecution or other legal proceedings shall lie against the Central Government or any officer of the Central Government or any member, officer or other employee of the Authority for anything which is in good faith done or intended to be done under this Act or the rules or regulations made there under:Provided that nothing in this Act shall exempt any person from any suit or other proceedings which might, apart from this Act, be brought against him.

23. Delegation of powers

(1) The Authority may, by general or special order in writing, delegate to the Chairperson or any other member or office of the Authority subject to such conditions, if any, as may be specified in the order such of its powers and functions under this Act as it may deem necessary.

(2) The Authority may, by a general or special order in writing, also form committees of the members and delegate to them the powers and functions of the Authority as may be specified by the regulations.

24. Power to make rules

(1) The Central Government may, by notification, make rules for carrying out the provisions of this Act.

(2) In particular, and without prejudice to the generality of the foregoing power, such rules may provide for all or any of the following matters, namely

(a) the salary and allowances payable to, and other terms and conditions of service of, the members other than part-time members under sub-section(1) of section 7

(b) The allowances to be paid to the part-time members under sub-section(2) of section 7;

(c) such other powers that may be exercised by the Authority under clause (q) of sub-section(2) of section 14;

(d) the form of annual statement of accounts to be maintained by the Authority under sub-section(1) of section 17;

(e) the form and the manner in which and the time within which returns and statements and particulars are to be furnished to the Central Government under sub-section(1) of section 20;

(f) the matters under sub-section(5) of section 25 on which the Insurance Advisory Committee shall advise the Authority;

(g) any other matter which is required to be, or may be, prescribed, or in respect of which provision is to be or may be made by rules.

25. Establishment of insurance advisory committee

(1) The Authority may, by notification, establish with effect from such date as it may specify in such notification, a Committee to be known as the Insurance Advisory Committee.

(2) The Insurance Advisory Committee shall consist of not more than twenty-five members excluding ex-officio members to represent the interests of commerce, industry, transport, agriculture, consumer for a, surveyors, agents, intermediaries, organizations engaged in safety and loss prevention, research bodies and employees' association in the insurance sector.

(3) The Chairperson and the members of the Authority shall be the ex officio Chairperson and ex officio members of the Insurance Advisory Committee.

(4) The objects of the Insurance Advisory Committee shall be to advise the Authority on matters relating to the making of the regulations under section 26.

(5) Without prejudice to the provisions of sub-section (4), the Insurance Advisory Committee may advise the Authority on such other matters as may be prescribed.

26. Power to make regulations

(1) The Authority may, in consultation with the Insurance Advisory Committee, by notification, make regulations consistent with this Act and the rules made thereunder to carry out the purposes of this Act.

(2) In particular, and without prejudice to the generality of the foregoing power, such regulations may provide for all or any of the following matters, namely :-

(a) the time and places of meetings of the Authority and the procedure to be followed at such meetings including the quorum necessary for the transaction of business under sub-section(1) of section 10;

(b) the transactions of business at its meetings under sub-section(4) of section 10;

(c) the terms and other conditions of service of officers and other employees of the Authority under sub-section(2) of section 12;

(d) the powers and functions which may be delegated to Committees of the members under sub-section(2) of section 23; and

(e) any other matter which is required to be, or may be, specified by regulations or in respect of which provision is to be or may be made by regulations.

27. Rules and regulations to be laid before parliament

Every rule and every regulation made under this Act shall be laid, as soon as may be after it is made, before each House of Parliament, while it is in session, for a total period of thirty days which may be comprised in one session or in two or more successive sessions, and if, before the expiry of the session immediately following the session or the successive session aforesaid, both Houses agree in making any, modification in the rule or regulation or both Houses agree that the rule or regulation should not be made, the rule or regulation shall thereafter have effect only in such modified form or be of no effect, as the case may be; so, however, that any such modification or annulment shall be without prejudice to the validity of anything previously done under that rule or regulation.

28. Application of other laws not barred

The provisions of this Act shall be in addition to, and not in derogation of, the provisions of any other law for the time being in force.

29. Power to remove difficulties

(1) If any difficulty arises in giving effect to the provisions of this Act, the Central Government may, by order published in the Official Gazette, make such provisions not inconsistent with the provisions of this Act as may appear to be necessary for removing the difficulty: Provided that no order shall be made under this section after the expiry of two years from the appointed day.

(2) Every order made under this section shall be laid, as soon as may be, after it is made, before each House of Parliament.

30. Amendment of act 4 of 1938

The Life Insurance Act, 1938 shall be amended in the manner specified in the First Schedule to this Act.

31. Amendment of act 31 of 1956

The Life Insurance Corporation Act, 1956 shall be amended in the manner specified in the Second Schedule to this Act.

32. Amendment of act 57 of 1972

The General Insurance Business (Nationalization) Act, 1972 shall be amended in the manner specified in the Third schedule to this Act.

General Insurance Act 1972

2.12 General Insurance Corporation of India (GIC)

Introduction

The General Insurance Business Nationalization Act was passed in 1972 to set up the general insurance business. It was the nationalization of 107 insurance companies into one main company called General Insurance Corporation of India and its four subsidiary companies with exclusive privilege for transacting general insurance business. This act has been amended and the exclusive privilege ceased on and from the commencement of the insurance regulatory and development authority act 1999. General Insurance Corporation has been working as a reinsurer in India. Their subsidiaries are working as a separate entity and plays significant role in the public sector of general insurance.

General insurance industry in India was nationalized and a government company known as General Insurance Corporation of India was formed by the central government in November, 1972. General insurance companies have willingly catered to these increasing demands and have offered a plethora of insurance covers that almost cover anything under the sun.

2.12.1 Objective of the GIC

- To carry on the general insurance business other than life, such as accident, fire etc.
- To aid and achieve the subsidiaries to conduct the insurance business and
- To help the conduct of investment strategies of the subsidiaries in an efficient and productive manner.

2.12.2 Role and Functions of GIC

- Carrying on of any part of the general insurance, if it thinks it is desirable to do so.
- Aiding, assisting and advising the acquiring companies in the matter of setting up of standards of conduct and sound practice in general insurance business.
- Rendering efficient services to policy holders of general insurance.
- Advising the acquiring companies in the matter of controlling

their expenses including the payment of commission and other expenses.

- Advising the acquiring companies in the matter of investing their fund.
- Issuing directives to the acquiring companies in relation to the conduct of general insurance business.
- Issuing directions and encouraging competition among the acquiring companies in order to render their services more efficiently.

2.12.3 Classification of Indian General Insurance Industry

General Insurance is also known as Non-Life Insurance in India. There are totally 16 General Insurance (Non-Life) Companies in India. These 16 General Insurance companies have been classified into two broad categories namely:

1. PSUs (Public Sector Undertakings)
2. Private Insurance Companies

2.12.4 PSUs (Public Sector Undertakings)

In India, Public Sector Undertakings (PSUs) play a significant role in the insurance sector. Here's a breakdown of the key PSU insurance companies:

General Insurance:

The New India Assurance Co. Ltd.:

A leading general insurance company in India.

National Insurance Co. Ltd.:

One of the oldest general insurance companies in the country.

The Oriental Insurance Co. Ltd.:

Provides a wide range of general insurance products.

United India Insurance Co. Ltd.:

Another major player in the general insurance market.

Agriculture Insurance Company of India Ltd. (AICIL):

Specializes in providing insurance coverage for the agricultural sector.

General Insurance Corporation of India (GIC Re):

This is the sole national reinsurer of India.

Life Insurance

Life Insurance Corporation of India (LIC):

The largest and most prominent life insurance company in India, and a major public sector undertaking.

2.12.5 Private Insurance Companies

The private insurance sector in India has seen significant growth since liberalization. Here's a look at some of the key private insurance companies, categorized for clarity:

Life Insurance

HDFC Life Insurance:

A prominent player offering a wide range of life insurance products.

ICICI Prudential Life Insurance:

One of the leading private life insurers in India.

SBI Life Insurance:

A major player with a strong network.

Max Life Insurance:

Known for its diverse life insurance solutions.

Bajaj Allianz Life Insurance:

Offers a comprehensive portfolio of life insurance plans.

Tata AIA Life Insurance:

A joint venture providing various life insurance options.

Kotak Mahindra Life Insurance:

Provides a range of life insurance and investment products.

PNB MetLife India Insurance:

Another major player in the life insurance sector.

General Insurance

ICICI Lombard General Insurance:

A leading general insurance company offering various non-life insurance products.

HDFC Ergo General Insurance:

Provides a wide range of general insurance solutions.

Bajaj Allianz General Insurance:

Offers diverse general insurance products.

Tata AIG General Insurance:

Provides various general insurance covers.

SBI General Insurance:

growing in the general insurance market.

Go Digit General Insurance:

A newer company that is very digitally focused.

Health Insurance:

Star Health and Allied Insurance:

Specializes in health insurance products.

Aditya Birla Health Insurance:

Offers a range of health insurance plans.

Care Health Insurance:

A company focused on health insurance products.

Niva Bupa Health Insurance:

Another company that is focused on providing health insurance.

ManipalCigna Health Insurance:

Provides health insurance solutions.

Chapter - 3

Insurance agent

3.1 Introduction

An insurance agent is a person who works for an insurance company and sells the insurance products of this company. An important aspect of working with an agent is that he / she sells insurance products of one company only, and thus is typically not able and not interested to compare prices and features of other products on the market. Agents should not be confused with brokers (or insurance brokers) who are typically able to compare products from several insurance providers.

Essential tips for success as an insurance agent

- Focus On Good Salesmanship.
- Develop a Strong Work Ethic.
- Study the Market.
- Meep Up with the Times.
- Learn From the Pros.
- Balance Work and Personal Ti

3.2 Essential Qualities of a Successful Insurance Agent

Communication Skills

One of the most important things to look for in an agent is their communication skills. Successful agents don't just sell insurance; they build relationships within customers. Open, honest communication is the key to establishing a long-lasting relationship between an agent and customer.

Organized

It is absolutely crucial that an insurance agent has good organizational skills. The insurance is a high-pressure industry. A successful agent is organized and efficient. They can work well under pressure and meets deadlines.

Punctual

No questions asked, an insurance agent must respect your time. If your agent can't show up on time to work, it's better to switch your agent.

Trust

Trust can make or break any relationship. Many insurance agents use deception to sell policies. It is extremely important that you hire a trustworthy, reliable insurance agent. Trust leads to business over time.

Flexible

Flexibility is another vital trait. Your insurance agent must be approachable and patient. Moreover, they should be able to cater to your changing insurance needs. Finding the right insurance agent can be tricky. Keep these factors in mind when interviewing potential insurance agents. Above all, make sure your agent can offer a wide range of insurance products from reputable insurance companies.

3.3 Procedure for becoming agent

Procedure for IRDA agent

Candidates should complete 50 hours of training from an IRDA approved training institution to act as Life or General Insurance agent. In case of Candidates who are seeking license for the first time to act as composite (i.e. Life & General) insurance agent has to complete 75 hours of training.

To be a LIC agent, your educational qualification should be at least 10th pass and the age should be minimum 18 years. Earlier, it was necessary to have 12th pass certificate to become an agent. Contact your nearest LIC branch office and meet the development officer there.

3.4 Types of Insurance agent

In India, the regulatory authority for the insurance sector is IRDAI, Insurance Regulatory and Development Authority of India. To explain the differences between the three main distribution channels for insurance:

1. Individual Insurance Agent

2. Captive Insurance Agent

3. Micro Finance Insurance Agents

Individual Insurance Agent

A person can become an individual agent, after taking the requisite training. Clear a certification examination. Then he/she gets licensed by IRDAI to sell insurance policies to the public. And provide services related to insurance. Including assisting at the time of a claim. This license may be for Life Insurance, General Insurance or both. One Insurance Agent can sell and represent, one particular life insurance company and one particular non-life insurance company, at the same time.

Captive Insurance Agent

Captive agents can sell insurance for one specific company, only. This particular insurance company is, typically, a "name brand" company. A Captive is a closely held Insurance Company. The main objective of its establishment is to insure the risks of its parent company and affiliated groups. Day-to-day operations are controlled by the owner company, which will also be the principal insured's. These day-to-day operations include underwriting and claim decisions as well as an investment policy of the captive.

Micro Finance Insurance Agents

According to IRDAI, A micro-insurance policy is like a Life or General Insurance policy. The maximum permissible limit for the Sum Assured is Rs 50,000.

3.5 Functions of Insurance agent

Functions of Insurance agent

An insurance agent may work in a team or individually. They have to deal with different people, such as team members, their seniors, and clients, and their work is usually target based.

All insurance agents have certain functions and duties, and a few of them are mentioned below:

- Take details of the client's requirements, understand it, and then suggest the appropriate insurance plan to the client.
- Calculate the premium details of the policy and discuss the same with the client.
- Attend programs, seminars, and meetings related to the field, and to learn about the latest techniques, products, and services.
- Call clients and policyholders to explain and deliver the insurance policy, to modify beneficiary, if asked, to estimate the insurance plan and recommend alterations or additions.
- Monitor insurance claims and make sure that they have settled rightfully for both the parties i.e., the insurer and the client.
- Discuss with clients what needs to be provided and receive information when the claims are made towards the insurance policies.
- Develop sales and marketing to compete with agents in the same field.
- Contact underwriters and customize insurance policies that will meet the client requirements, covering multiple risks, to make sure that the given plan suits the client's insurance needs.
- To get customers to complete essential medical test requirements and completing KYC formalities.
- Examine and inspect the overall condition of the property, type of construction, age, and other characteristics to help underwriters in their decisions, whether it is an appropriate insurance risk for both the customer and the insurance company.
- Explain the features, merits, and demerits of various insurance policies to encourage the sale of an insurance policy.
- Interview potential customers to gather data about their insurance needs, financial resources, future financial requirements, the physical condition of the person (in case of

life insurance), or property (in case of general insurance) to be insured and know about their existing coverage, if any.

- Plan and review the integration of insurance policies into the accounting system of the company.
- Carry out certain administrative tasks like handling policy renewals.
- Market and sell different types of insurance plans to individuals, businesses, and groups on behalf of the insurance company.
- Constantly look for new clients and increase the network to find out new customers.
- Work on the allotted sales target and obtain the same by adopting various methods and strategies.
- Understand the client's requirement and if required, request the higher authorities to customize the insurance plan to meet the customer's requirements.
- An insurance agent continually needs to keep himself updated about policy-related information such as modification in the existing plan, or services or the introduction of a new policy.
- Collect information regarding the other insurance companies and know about their products and services. This helps an insurance agent to explain the clients and how their insurance plans are competent as compared to others.

3.6 Suspension of Appointment of an Agent

Suspension of Appointment of an Agent:

1)The appointment of an agent may be cancelled or suspendedafter due notice and after giving him/her a reasonable opportunity f being heard if he/she:-

a) violates the provisions of the Insurance Act,1938 (4 of 1938), Insurance Regulatory and Development Authority Act, 1999 (41 of 1999) or rules or regulations, made there under as amended from time to time;

b) Attracts any of the disqualifications mentioned in Clause VII.

c) Fails to comply with the code of conduct stipulated in Clause VIII and directions issued by the Authority from time to time.

d) Violates terms of appointment.

e) Fails to furnish any information relating to his/her activities as an agent as required by the Insurer or the Authority;

f) Fails to comply with the directions issued by the Authority;

g) Furnishes wrong or false information; or conceals or fails to disclose material facts in the application submitted for appointment of Agent or during the period of its validity.

h) Does not submit periodical returns as required by the Insurer/Authority;

i)does not co-operate with any inspection or enquiry conducted by the Authority;

j) fails to resolve the complaints of the policyholders or fails to give a satisfactory reply to the Authority in this behalf;

3.7 Documentation Requirements for getting license

Documentation Requirements for getting license

1. Application Form duly completed and declaration duly signed by at least two directors/partners.
2. Demand draft against the License Fee.,
3. Memorandum of Association and Article of Association of the company (In case of the company) or Partnership Deed in case of partnership firm.
4. Audited Balance Sheet of the Company

5. Proof of Fixed Deposit with any Scheduled Bank as required by the regulation.

6. Detailed Statement of Shareholding pattern of the company, containing the names of the shareholders, number of shares held, share certificate numbers and folio numbers; duly verified and certified by the auditor.

7. IT returns for last 3 years of Individual shareholders along-with their net worth certificates and affidavit regarding the source of invested funds.

8. Annual reports of the shareholder companies for last 3 years.

9. Board resolution of the shareholder company regarding the investment in the said company.

10. Auditors certificate regarding NBFC status of the shareholding company

11. If share holding company is an NBFC (Non-banking finance company), then No Objection Certificate from RBI NA

12. Detailed CV and attested testimonials including training certificate of the Principal Officer.

13. Detailed CV and testimonials of the key managerial persons.

14. Details of the persons qualified and trained along-with their testimonials and training certificates.

15. List of persons responsible for procuring insurance business alongwith their testimonials.

16. Necessary proof of infrastructure, office space, trained manpower etc.

17. List of prospective clients with expected premium.

18. Business and income projection for next 3 years with class wise breakup.

19. Projected Revenue account, profit and loss account and balance sheet for next 3 years.

20. Detailed organization chart mentioning roles and responsibilities. (Pg 200)

21. Affidavit regarding non-suffering from any disqualification under Section 42 D of the Insurance Act.

22. Undertaking regarding non-holding of any Directorship/employment in any other insurance entity by the Director/employees of the company.

23. Undertaking regarding non-holding of any agency/surveyor/TPA license by any director/employee

24. Undertaking that in the past no person connected to the applicant has been denied license by the authority

25. Undertaking by the Principal Officer regarding non-violation of the code of conduct

26. Undertaking that the applicant is not engaged in any other business other than the objectives of the applicant as mentioned in MOA/Partnership deed.

27. If JV, copy of agreement with partner/s

Points To Check

1. Whether it has the word 'Broker/Broking' in its name.

2. MOA contains the insurance broking as its main objective.

3. Whether the company fulfills the minimum Capital requirement in the manner provided for in the Regulations.

4. It has no foreign capital exceeding 26% of the total paid up capital.

5. Whether the Fixed Deposit of 20% of initial capital is made in a scheduled bank.

6. The principal officer has the adequate Qualification, passed the Brokers exam and has acquired requisite training.

7. The company engages at least two persons with the required qualification and training.

8. It has sufficient infrastructure and trained manpower to run the insurance broking business.

9. The persons responsible for procuring insurance business are qualified and trained.

3.8 IRDA License

Until the year 1999, the insurance sector in India was controlled by the Controller of Insurance under the Insurance Act, 1938. However, the formation of IRDA made felt the need of renaissance in the sector of insurance as most of the earlier provisions were outdated and irrelevant in the present context.

3.8.1 Scope of IRDA License

The new IRDA regulations covered the following points of importance in the field of insurance:

- The procedure of obtaining license of insurance from IRDA;
- The procedure of obtaining approval of insurance products from IRDA
- The procedure for appointment of insurance intermediary.

3.8.2 Procedure of granting license to companies to start insurance business

It is mandatory for every entity to obtain a Certificate from Authority before carrying on any insurance business. The license for various classes of insurance can be obtained from IRDA, such as Life Insurance, Fire Insurance, Marine Insurance etc. But it is to be kept in mind that the life insurance business shall not be combined with any other type of insurance business.

The license from IRDA is mandatory. Even the old players in the field of insurance, such as National Insurance, General Insurance, Oriental Insurance etc., had to obtain a fresh certificate within 3months from the date of commencement of this Act. The insurers exempted from obtaining license under the previous Act, were covered under this Act

3.8.3 Application for Registration Certificate before IRDA

First Stage

An application for the Certificate of Registration shall be made to the IRDA in prescribed Form IRDA/R1. The application shall be supported by the following documents:

The certified copy of the Memorandum of Association and Articles of Association;

The full profile including the name, address and occupation of all the directors and shareholders of the company;

The statement regarding the class of insurance business proposed to be carried on.

The statement regarding the sources of capital funds.

The initial application will be screened by IRDA and additional information may be asked for. Even a Principal Officer may be appointed by the Authority for seeking any information or clarification on their behalf.

Second Stage

Once being satisfied about the information and documents provided along with the Form IRDA/R1, the Authority may ask for an additional application in the prescriber Form IRDA/R2 which shall be accompanied with the following documents:

Every entity shall deposit either in cash or in securities, partly in cash and party in securities, the following:

1. 1% of the total gross premium written in India in the previous year, in case of the life insurance business, not exceeding INR 10 crore;

2. 3% of the total gross premium written in India in the previous year, in case of the general insurance business, not exceeding INR 10 crore;

3. A sum of INR 20 crores in case of reinsurance business;

4. A sum of INR 1 lac/- only in case of marine business;

5. The certificate showing the amount deposited with the Reserve Bank of India.

The statement showing declaration from the Principal Officer about fulfillment of Minimum Capital Requirement. The capital requirement shall be 20 crores for reinsurance business and 10 crores for the life insurance and General Insurance.

A copy of the certified public prospectus and the policy reforms of the insurer.

Statement depicting assured rate, advantages, terms & conditions associated with Insurance policies.

Actuary certificate regarding rate of interest.

A deposit of INR 50,000/- for each class of business.

If any foreign promoter is involved, then the certified copy of the MOU between the Indian and Foreign promoter.

Any other document asked for by the authority.

3.8.4 Grant of Registration Certificate for Insurance business in India

After the receipt of application and on being satisfied about the following mentioned conditions, the Certificate of Registration shall be granted to the insurer by the IRDA. The conditions include the following:

Sound financial condition and general character of the management;

Adequate volume, capital structure and earning prospects of the applicant company;

Fulfillment of the interest of the general public.

3.8.5 Refusal of Registration for insurance operations

The applicant may be refused of the registration of an insurer on the following grounds:

Inadequate or improper information;

Delay in providing information;

Non-fulfillment of capital requirements;

Improper conduct of the management;

Any other as decided by the Authority.

If the applicant is refused of the registration as an insurer, he can appeal before the Central Govt. within 30 days from the date on which a copy of the decision from the Authority is received

In case of the insurance registration, the decision of the government shall be final and cannot be appealed against in any court of law.

3.8.6 Cancellation of Registration

In case any of the conditions specified for registration is not compiled with, then the Authority reserves the right to cancel the registration either wholly or in part, in case the applicant is involved in more than one insurance business.

3.8.7 Renewal of Registration

The registration for insurance shall be renewed every year and the application for renewal shall be made before 31st December of the preceding year following which the renewal is sought for, along with the fees as below:

1/4th of the 1% of the premium received during the year or INR 5 crores, whichever is less;

The fees should not be less than 50,000/- for each class of insurance;

1/4th of the 1% of the premium received during the year in India, for reinsurance companies;

The renewal fees shall be paid to the Reserve Bank of India.

3.8.8 Remuneration to agent

The insurance statutory and regulatory framework has, historically, strictly restricted the amount of commission or remuneration that can be paid to insurance agents and insurance intermediaries (such as insurance brokers, corporate agents, web aggregators and insurance marketing firms) for the solicitation and procurement of insurance business. Apart from overall commission caps contained in §40A of the Insurance Act 1938, regulations and guidelines applicable to insurance intermediaries such as the IRDAI (Insurance Brokers) Regulations 2013, the IRDAI's Licensing of Corporate Agents Guidelines of 14th July 2005 and the IRDA (Web Aggregators) Regulations 2013 also placed restrictions on the commission/remuneration that could be paid to insurance intermediaries for placing insurance business.

Manner and conditions for payment of commission or remuneration to insurance agents and insurance intermediaries and for payment of renewal commission and hereditary commission to insurance agents/their legal heirs after the termination of the insurance agency.

- Manner and conditions for payment of reward to insurance agents and insurance intermediaries which is "over and above the commission or remuneration" but cannot exceed:
- 20% of the first year commission or remuneration in the case of

individual insurance agents;

- 40% of the first year commission or remuneration in the case of insurance intermediaries.
- Manner and conditions regarding the transfer of orphan policies.
- Grounds and manner for the termination, suspension and cancellation of the appointment of insurance agents and insurance intermediaries.
- Any restrictions on the products to be sold by insurance agents or insurance intermediaries.
- The Board approved policy is to be reviewed annually and changes, if any, are to be filed with the IRDAI within 30 days of the change.
- The Draft Regulations supersede the commission limits specified in the Products Regulations for products to be introduced. However, for all existing products, the commission limits specified by the Products Regulations and the limits set out in the IRDAI approved File & Use application for General Insurers shall continue to be the maximum limits for commission.
- The Draft Regulations clarify that where policies are procured "directly" by the Insurer, no commission or remuneration is payable, leaving the question open in terms of whether any commission, remuneration or reward is payable on products
- Designated as "Online" products which are attributed to the Insurer's direct channel, but may be displayed on a broker or web aggregator's website.
- Insurers are required to file a return in the specified format of the commission, remuneration and rewards paid each financial year that must be certified by the CEO, CFO, CCO and the statutory auditors of the Insurer.

3.8.9 Code of conduct and unfair practices

VII. Disqualification to act as an Insurance Agent: The conditions for disqualification shall be as stipulated under Section 42 (3) of the Act.

VIII. Code of Conduct.

1) Every agent, shall adhere to the code of conduct specified below:-

a) Every insurance agent shall,---

i) identify himself and the insurer of whom he is an insurance agent;

ii) show the agency identity card to the prospect, and also disclose the agency appointment letter to the prospect on demand;

iii) disseminate the requisite information in respect of insurance products offered for sale by his insurer and take into account the needs of the prospect while recommending a specific insurance plan;

iv) where the Insurance agent represents more than one insurer offering same line of products, he should dispassionately advice the policyholder on the products of all Insurers whom he is representing and the product best suited to the specific needs of the prospect.

v) disclose the scales of commission in respect of the insurance product offered for sale, if asked by the prospect;

vi) indicate the premium to be charged by the insurer for the insurance product offered for sale;

vii) explain to the prospect the nature of information required in the proposal form by the insurer, and also the importance of disclosure of material information in the purchase of an insurance contract;

viii) bring to the notice of the insurer every fact about the prospect relevant to insurance underwriting, including any adverse habits or income inconsistency of the prospect, within the knowledge of the agent, in the form of a report called "Insurance Agent's Confidential Report" along with every proposal submitted to the insurer wherever applicable, and any material fact that may adversely affect the underwriting decision of the insurer as regards acceptance of the proposal, by making all reasonable enquiries about the prospect;

ix) obtain the requisite documents at the time of filing the proposal form with the insurer; and other documents subsequently asked for by the insurer for completion of the proposal;

x) advise every prospect to effect nomination under the policy

xi) inform promptly the prospect about the acceptance or rejection of the proposal by the insurer;

xii) render necessary assistance and advice to every policyholder on all policy servicing matters including assignment of policy, change of address or exercise of options under the policy or any other policy service, wherever necessary;

xiii) render necessary assistance to the policyholders or claimants or beneficiaries in complying with the requirements for settlement of claims by the insurer;

2) No insurance agent shall

a) solicit or procure insurance business without being appointed to act as such by the insurer

b) induce the prospect to omit any material information in the proposal form;

c) induce the prospect to submit wrong information in the proposal form or documents submitted to the insurer for acceptance of the proposal;

d) resort to multilevel marketing for soliciting and procuring insurance policies and/or induct any prospect/policyholder to join a multilevel level marketing scheme.

e) behave in a discourteous manner with the prospect;

f) interfere with any proposal introduced by any other insurance agent;

g) offer different rates, advantages, terms and conditions other than those offered by his insurer;

h) demand or receive a share of proceeds from the beneficiary under an insurance contract;

i) force a policyholder to terminate the existing policy and to effect a new policy from him within three years from the date of such termination of the earlier policy;

j) apply for fresh agency appointment to act as an insurance agent, if his agency appointment was earlier cancelled by the designated official, and a period of five years has elapsed from the date of such cancellation;

k) Become or remain a director of any insurer

3) Every insurance agent shall, with a view to conserve the insurance business already procured through him, make every attempt to ensure remittance of the premiums by the policyholders within the stipulated time, by giving notice to the policyholder orally and in writing;

4) Any person who acts as an insurance agent in contravention of the provisions of this Act shall be liable to a penalty which may extend to ten thousand rupees and any insurer or any person acting on behalf of an insurer, who appoints any person as an insurance agent not permitted to act as such or transact any insurance business in India through any such person shall be liable to penalty which may extend to one crore rupees.

5) The insurer shall be responsible for all acts and omissions of its agents including violation of code of conduct specified under these guidelines, and shall be liable to a penalty which may extend to one crore rupees.

IX. Authority's right to inspect

1) The Authority may appoint one or more of its officers as an "Investigating Officer" to undertake inspection of affairs of an insurance Agent, to ascertain and see whether the business is carried on by him/her as per the Act, Regulations and the instructions issued by the Authority from time to time, and also to inspect the books of accounts, records and documents of the Agent.

Provided such inspection will be limited to the matters pertaining to insurance business undertaken by the Insurance Agent.

2) The Investigating Officer may, during the course of the inspection, examine on oath the insurance agent or any person who is found to be in possession or control of any books, accounts or other documents, and any statement made by the insurance agent or such person during such examination may thereafter be used as evidence in any proceedings under these Guidelines.

3) The Authority may also call for any information from the insurance agent and he shall submit the same within the time lines referred therein by the Authority.

4) The purposes of inspection under this Clause may include but are not limited to ;-

a) Monitoring compliance with the provisions of the Act, rules, regulations etc.

b) Investigation of the complaints of serious nature received from any insured, any insurers, other stakeholders or any other individual on any matter having a bearing on the insurance related activities of the Agent; and

c) Investigating into the affairs of the Insurance Agent in the interest of proper development of insurance business or in protection of policyholder's interest.

X. Suspension of Appointment of an Agent

1) The appointment of an agent may be cancelled or suspended after due notice and after giving him/her a reasonable opportunity of being heard if he/she:-

a) violates the provisions of the Insurance Act,1938 (4 of 1938), Insurance Regulatory and Development Authority Act, 1999 (41 of 1999) or rules or regulations, made there under as amended from time to time;

b) attracts any of the disqualifications mentioned in Clause VII.

c) Fails to comply with the code of conduct stipulated in Clause VIII and directions issued by the Authority from time to time.

d) Violates terms of appointment.

e) Fails to furnish any information relating to his/her activities as an agent as required by the Insurer or the Authority;

f) Fails to comply with the directions issued by the Authority;

g) Furnishes wrong or false information; or conceals or fails to disclose material facts in the application submitted for appointment of Agent or during the period of its validity.

h) does not submit periodical returns as required by the Insurer/Authority;

i) does not co-operate with any inspection or enquiry conducted by the Authority;

j) fails to resolve the complaints of the policyholders or fails to give a satisfactory reply to the Authority in this behalf;

XI. Manner of holding enquiry before/after suspension of appointment of the insurance Agent:

1. The appointment of an insurance agent shall not be cancelled unless an enquiry has been conducted in accordance with the procedure specified in this clause.

2. For the purpose of holding an enquiry under this clause, the insurer may appoint an Officer as an Enquiry Officer within 15 days of the issue of the suspension order;

3. The Enquiry Officer shall issue a show cause notice to the insurance agent at the registered address of the insurance agent calling for all information / data as deemed necessary to conduct the enquiry and grant the insurance agent a time of 21 days from date of receipt of the show cause notice, for submission of his/her reply and such information / data called for;

4. The insurance Agent may, within 21 days from the date of receipt of such notice, furnish to the enquiry officer a reply to the Show cause notice together with copies of documentary or other evidence relied on by him or sought by the Enquiry Officer;

5. The Enquiry Officer shall give a reasonable opportunity of hearing to the insurance agent to enable him to make submissions in support of his/her reply;

6. The insurance agent may either appear in person or through any person duly authorised by him to present his case, provided however that the prior approval of the Insurer is obtained for the appearance of the 'Authorised Person';

7. If it is considered necessary, the Enquiry Officer may require the Insurer to present its case through one of its officers;

8. If it is considered necessary, the Enquiry Officer may call for feedback/information from any other related entity during the course of enquiry;

9. If it is considered necessary, the Enquiry Officer may call for additional papers from the insurance agent;

10. The Enquiry Officer shall make all necessary efforts to complete the proceeding at the earliest but in no case beyond 45 days of the commencement of the enquiry:

Provided that in case the enquiry cannot be completed within the prescribed time limit of 45 days as mentioned in (10) above; the enquiry officer may seek additional time from the Insurer stating the reason thereof;

11. The Enquiry Officer shall, after taking into account all relevant facts and submissions made by the insurance agent, shall furnish a report making his/her recommendations to the Designated Official. The Designated Official shall pass a final order in writing with reasons. The order of designated official shall be signed and dated and communicated to the agent.

Chapter – 4

Life Insurance

Meaning

Life Insurance is defined as a contract between the policy holder and the insurance company, where the life insurance company pays a specific sum to the insured individual's family upon his death. The life insurance sum is paid in exchange for a specific amount of premium.

Features of Life Insurance

Policyholder

Policyholder is the individual who pays the premium for the life insurance policy and signs a life insurance contract with a life insurance company.

Premium

A premium is the cost the policyholder pays the life insurance company for covering his/her life.

Maturity

Maturity is the stage at which the policy term is completed and the life insurance contract ends.

Insured

Insured is the individual whose life is secured via the life insurance . After his/her death the insurance company is accountable to provide a financial amount to the dependents.

Sum Assured

The amount the insurance company pays the dependents of the insured if those events occur which are specified in the life insurance contract.

Policy Term

Policy term is the specified duration (listed in the life insurance contract) for which the insurance company provides a life cover and the time period during which the contract is active (listed in the life insurance contract).

Nominee

A nominee is an individual listed in the life insurance contract who is entitled to receive the predetermined compensation, as a part of the policy.

Claim

On the insured's demise, the nominees can file a claim with the insurance provider in order to receive the predetermined payout amount

4.2 Advantages of Life Insurance

Advantages of life Insurance

Death Benefits

Life insurance enables individuals to protect themselves and their families, in case of any unfortunate happening in the life of the insurer. The insurer pays an amount equivalent to the sum assured as specified in the contract along with applicable bonuses. This is know as the death benefit.

Investment Components

Certain whole life insurance policies offer two pronged benefits of both insurance and investment. While one half of your premium is paid toward insurance, the other half is invested in equity, debt or combinations of both. You get the best of both worlds with a protective covering as well as high returns on your investments. You can make the most of this component by investing in funds that align with your investment horizon and risk appetite. Certain policies allow you to switch between funds as per your evolving goals. The Invest 4G plan offered by Canara HSBC Oriental Bank of Commerce gives you the option of choosing from a range of 7 unit-linked funds and 4 different portfolio management options as per your preference.

Maturity Benefits

Life insurance policies can also double as a savings instrument by offering maturity benefits. If the insured survives the policy term and no claims have been made, the total premiums paid are returned at the time of maturity of the policy. In this manner, your life insurance plan can have a savings component, while also offering a protective cover.

Tax Benefits

Under the umbrella of Section 80C of the Income Tax Act (ITA), individuals can reduce their tax liabilities by investing in specific instruments. Term insurance is one of them. Under section 80C, the premium paid for your life insurance policy is eligible to attain a maximum tax deduction for up to Rs. 1.5 lakh. In addition to this, under Section 10(10D), any payouts you receive from your insurance policy are completely tax-free (provided your premium does not exceed 10% of your Sum Assured, annually). If you have opted for a health-related rider, such as a critical illness or surgical care rider, you can also avail tax deductions under 80D of the ITA.

Coverage against Liabilities

To fulfill your dreams and attain your goals, you may have required a certain amount of financial support - in the form of loans, mortgages and other types of debt. Be it student loans or credit card debt, dealing with such liabilities can be a source of great financial strain, without a steady stream of income. While you may have the funds to pay off a part of your loans now, your family may find it difficult to manage such liabilities in the event of your unfortunate demise, owing to the loss of income. Thus, taking a life insurance policy ensures that your family has the financial means to steadily meet your loan and mortgage repayments, even in your absence.

Riders

You can opt for riders to enhance your life insurance coverage. A number of riders, ranging from Critical Illness to Accidental Total Permanent Disability are available and help protect you and your loved ones against instances where in your life cover may not come into play.

4.3 Principles of Life Insurance

Principles of Life Insurance

There are broadly four major insurance principles applied in India, these being

- Insurable Interest – This principle pertains to the level of interest an individual is expected to have in a particular policy.

The interest could be a family bond, a personal relationship and so on. Based on the interest level, an insurance company can choose to accept or reject an application in order to protect the misuse of a policy.

- Law of large numbers – This is a theory that ensures long-term stability and minimises losses in the long run when experiments are done with large numbers.
- Good faith – Purchasing an insurance is entering into a contract between company and individual. This should be done in good faith by providing all relevant details with honesty. Covering any information from the insurance company may result in serious consequences for the individual in the future. This being said, the insurer must explain all aspects of a policy and ensure that there are no unexplained or hidden clauses and that the applicant is made aware of all terms and conditions.
- Risk & Minimal loss – Insurance is a risky and companies have to do business and make profits keeping in mind the risk factor. The principle of minimal risk states that the insured individual is expected to take necessary action to limit him/her self from any hazards. This includes following a healthy lifestyle, getting a regular health check-up and more.

4.4 Merits of Life Insurance

1. Risk Coverage: Insurance provides risk coverage to the insured family in form of monetary compensation in lieu of premium paid.

2. Difference plans for different uses: Insurance companies offer a different type of plan to the insured depending on his need for insurance. More benefits come with the more premium.

3. Cover for Health Expenses: These policies also cover hospitalization expenses and critical illness treatment.

4. Promotes Savings/ Helps in Wealth creation: Insurance policies also come with the saving plan i.e. they invest your money in profitable ventures.

5. Guaranteed Income: Insurance policies come with the guaranteed sum assured amount which is payable on happening of the event.

6. Loan Facility: Insurance companies provide the option to the insured that they can borrow a certain sum of amount. This option is available on selected policies only.

7. Tax Benefits: Insurance premium is tax deductible under section 80C of the income tax Act, 1961.

4.5 Demerits of Life Insurance

1. Policyholders forego some current expenditure to pay policy premiums. Moreover, life insurance is typically purchased for the benefit of others and usually only indirectly for the insured person.

2. Cash surrender values are usually less than the premiums paid in the first several policy years and sometimes a policy owner may not recover the premiums paid if the policy is surrendered.

3. The life insurance purchase decision and the positioning of the life insurance can be complex especially if the insurance is for estate planning, business situations or complex family situations.

4. The life insurance acquisition process can be annoying and perplexing (e.g. Is the life insurance agent trustworthy? Is this the right product and carrier? How can medical underwriting be streamlined?

4.6 Types of Life Insurance Policies

Types of life insurance policies

- **Term life**
- **permanent life**

Types of Life Insurance

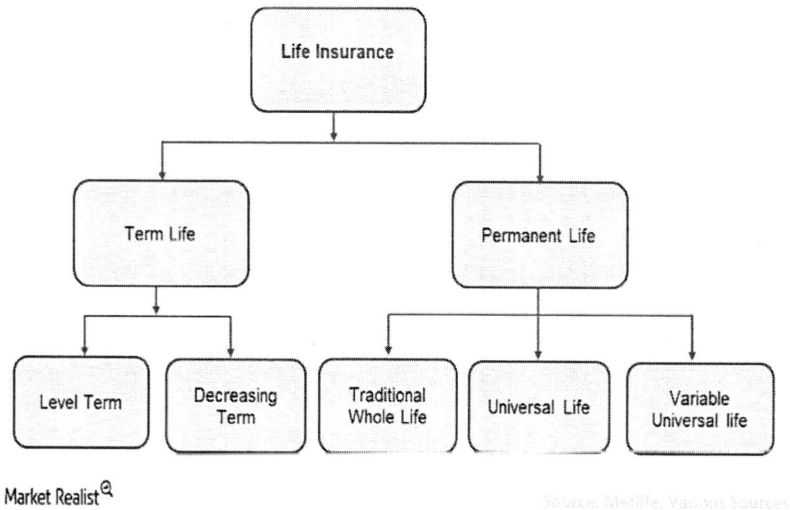

These two types are further sub-divided into other types of policies as discussed below.

Term Policies

A term policy is a simple product that provides insurance (VFH) (IYF) coverage for a specified period. If the policyholder dies during this period, the beneficiaries receive the death benefits. The premium for the policy is based on the insured person's age and health. Term policy has no investment component. There are two basic types of term life policies

Level term: The death benefits remain the same throughout the life of the policy.

Decreasing term: The death benefits decline over the life of the policy.

Permanent Policies

Permanent policies provide lifetime death benefit coverage with a cash value component. We'll discuss cash value accumulation in detail in the next article.

The permanent life insurance policies are usually categorized into three types

- Traditional whole life insurance
- Universal life insurance
- Variable universal life insurance

4.7 Claims of Life Insurance

Claims of Life Insurance (Settlement Process)

Formalities for a death claim

When a person with a life insurance policy – called a life assured – dies, claim intimation should be sent to the insurance company as early as possible. The assignee or nominee under the policy can do this. So can any close relative or the agent who handles the policy.

The claim intimation should contain information like the date, place and cause of death. The insurance agent has the duty to help the life assured's family/ assignee to deal with the insurance company to fulfil the formalities for a claim.

The insurance company will respond to this intimation and will ask for the following documents:

- Filled-up claim form (provided by the insurance company)
- Certificate of death
- Policy document
- Deeds of assignments/ re-assignments if any
- Legal evidence of title, if the policy is not assigned or nominated

Form of discharge executed and witnessed Other documents such as medical attendant's certificate, hospital certificate, employer's certificate, police inquest report, post mortem report etc could be called for, as applicable.

4.7.1 Formalities for a maturity claim

Where a life insurance policy is maturing, the insurance company will usually send intimation to the policyholder along with a discharge voucher at least two to three months in advance of the date of maturity giving details like the maturity amount payable.

The policyholder has to sign the discharge voucher – which is like a receipt – have his signature witnessed and send it back to the insurance company along with the original policy bond to enable it to make the payment.

If the policy has been assigned in favour of any other person or entity – like a housing loan company – the claim amount will be paid only to the assignee who will give the discharge.

4.8 Life Insurance Companies in India

Some of the prominent life insurance companies in India are:

1. LIC – life insurance Corporation of India

2. SBI Life Insurance

3. ICICI Prudential Life Insurance

4. HDFC Standard Life Insurance

5. Bajaj Allianz Life Insurance

6. Max Life Insurance

7. Birla Sun Life Insurance

8. Kotak Life Insurance

4.9 Surrender Value

Meaning

The cash surrender value is defined as the accumulated component of an insurance policy that is paid if you cancel the same. You need to remember that the surrender value is available on traditional insurance plans such as whole life or endowment plans. Surrender value is not applicable if you purchase a term plan.

Definition of Surrender Value

It is the amount the policyholder will get from the life insurance company if he decides to exit the policy before maturity - Economic times. Cashing out on your life insurance

When you surrender your life insurance plan, you are canceling the coverage and availing of the accumulated cash value. When you cash out on the insurance policy, the insurance company levies certain charges. These charges are reduced from the accumulated cash value on your policy. Before deciding to surrender your insurance, you need to remember that the result will be the loss of life coverage. If you require money, you may consider borrowing against your life insurance policy.

4.9.1 Cashing out versus borrowing against your life insurance policy

When contemplating the surrender value in insurance, you may refer to one of the two following ideas:

1. The investment value you will receive when you surrender your policy in lieu of the life coverage offered under the plan. When you choose this option, your nominees do not receive any policy benefits in case of an unfortunate event as you decide to cash out the accumulated value on the same before its maturity.

2. The amount you may be able to borrow against your insurance coverage during its duration.Under this option, you can avail of cash on your policy without foregoing the insurance coverage. Generally, the interest rate on such borrowed amount is low and affordable.Both the aforementioned options allow you to avail of cash on your insurance policy albeit in different ways.Both the aforementioned options allow you to avail of cash on your insurance policy albeit in different ways.

How does 'cash value' work in a life insurance policy?

To understand how to calculate cash surrender value of life insurance, you need to comprehend its working. You pay a premium to procure insurance coverage. A portion of this premium is used towards providing the life coverage and administrative fees and the balance is invested by the insurer on your behalf. This portion earns returns through such investments, which are then provided as accumulated benefits.

How is the cash value of a life insurance policy calculated?

The cash value in a life policy accumulates over the years. Therefore, when you pay the premiums regularly for a longer period, the cash value of the policy increases. This is because the investible component of the premium has a longer time to grow. To know what is surrender value in insurance, it is recommended you ask your financial advisor or directly procure the calculation from the insurer. You also need to know the surrender period. It is the period that you need to wait before the policy has a cash surrender value

Surrender fees

Another aspect is the surrender fees charged by the insurer when you cancel the policy or withdraw funds prematurely. It is higher during the initial years and reduces as time passes.Before you decide to surrender the policy, it is recommended you ask the insurer if you can withdraw the cash surrender value and use some portion to buy a less expensive policy. You may choose to surrender your policy as you may not need it or want to purchase a new one. It is an important decision and you need to consider all factors before making your choice.

4.10 Fire Insurance

Meaning

The term fire in fire insurance is interpreted in the literal and popular sense. There is fire when something burns. In other words fire means visible flames or actual ignition. Simmering/ smouldering are not considered fire in Fire Insurance. Fire produces heat and light but either of them alone is not fire. Lightening is not a fire but if itignites something,the damage may be due to fire.

Definition

Under section 2(6A) Insurance Act 1938, the fire insurance business is defined as follows: "Fire insurance business means the business of effecting, otherwise than independently to some other class of business, contracts of insurance against loss by or incidental to fire or other occurrence customarily included among the risks insured against in fire insurance policies".

4.11 Features of Fire Insurance

1) Offer & Acceptance: It is a prerequisite to any contract. Similarly, the property will be insured under fire insurance policy after the offer is accepted by the insurance company. Example: A proposal submitted to the insurance company along with premium on 1/1/2011 but the insurance company accepted the proposal on 15/1/2011. The risk is covered from 15/1/2011 and any loss prior to this date will not be covered under fire insurance.

2) Payment of Premium: An owner must ensure that the premium is paid well in advance so that the risk can be covered. If the payment is made through cheque and it is dishonored then the coverage of risk will not exist. It is as per section 64VB of Insurance Act 1938. (Details under insurance legislation Module).

3) Contract of Indemnity: Fire insurance is a contract of indemnity and the insurance company is liable only to the extent of actual loss suffered. If there is no loss, there is no liability even if there is fire. Example: If the property is insured for Rs 20 lakhs under fire insurance and it is damaged by fire to the extent of Rs. 10 lakhs, then the insurance company will not pay more than Rs. 10 lakhs.

4) Utmost Good Faith: The property owner must disclose all the relevant information to the insurance company while insuring their property. The fire policy shall be voidable in the event of misrepresentation, mis-description or non-disclosure of any material information. Example: The use of building must be disclosed i.e whether the building is used for residential use or manufacturing use, as in both the cases the premium rate will vary.

5) Insurable Interest: The fire insurance will be valid only if the person who is insuring the property is owner or having insurable interest in that property. Such interest must exist at the time when loss occurs. It is well known that insurable interest exists not only with the ownership but also as a tenant or bailee or financier. Banks can also have the insurable interest. Example: Mr. A is the owner of the building. He insured that building and later on sold the building to Mr. B and the fire took place in the building. Mr. B will not get the compensation from the insurance company because he has not taken the insurance policy

being a owner of the property. After selling to Mr. B, Mr. A has no insurable interest in the property.

6) Contribution: If a person insured his property with two insurance companies, then in case of fire loss both the insurance companies will pay the loss to the owner proportionately. Example: A property worth Rs. 50 lakhs was insured with two Insurance companies A and B. In case of loss, both insurance companies will contribute equally.

7) Period of fire Insurance: The period of insurance is to be defined in the policy. Generally the period of fire insurance will not exceed by one year. The period can be less than one year but not more than one year except for the residential houses which can be insured for the period exceeding one year also.

8) Deliberate Act: If a property is damaged or loss occurs due to fire because of deliberate act of the owner, then that damage or loss will not be covered under the policy.

9) Claims: To get the compensation under fire insurance the owner must inform the insurance company immediately so that the insurance company can take necessary steps to determine the loss.

4.12 Types of Fire Insurance Policy

Some Important Types of Fire Insurance Policy in India

Specific fire insurance policy: In this type of fire insurance in India a specified sum insured amount id selected for a specific property for a specified period. The total actual loss does not go past the sum insured amount.

Comprehensive policy: This type of fire insurance policy offers full protection that encompasses a range of risks such as theft, riot, pest related damage, lighting, civil commotion aside from fire related risks.

Valued policy: This type of fire insurance policy is named such because the property value is worked out at the beginning and the coverage is determined according to the value of the property and not the market value. Both the insured and the insurer agreed upon the value before the fire insurance policy starts to have effect.

Floating policy: This type of fire insurance policy covers multiple goods owned by the same person at a time for one premium and sum assured.

Valuable Policy: In valuable fire insurance policy, market price of damaged property determines the claim amount.One should compare fire insurance to select the right type of fire insurance policy out of all the variants available in the market. One should compare fire insurance to select the right type of fire insurance policy out of all the variants available in the market.

Procedure to insure the property under fire insurance

1) Filling of proposal form

2) Inspection of the property

3) Payment of premium

4) Issue of Cover note/ Policy document in lieu of acceptance of the proposal

Procedure to Settle the Fire Insurance Claim

A) If there is any damage or loss arising due to fire then the policy holder should immediately inform the insurance company in writing and with estimated amount of loss.

B) Survey Report: If the amount of loss is small (i.e. up to Rs. 20,000/-), the insurance company may depute an officer to survey the loss and decide on the settlement of the loss on the basis of the claim form and the officer's report. However, in large losses, an independent surveyor duly licensed by the Government is appointed to give a report on the loss.

The survey report would generally deal with the following matters:

(i) Cause of loss.

(ii) Extent of loss.

(iii) Under-Insurance, if any..

(iv) Details and value of salvage, and how it has been disposed of or proposed to be disposed of.

(v) Details of expenses (e.g. fire brigade expenses).

(vi) Compliance with policy conditions and warranties.

(vii) Details of other insurance policies on the same property, and the apportionment of the loss and expenses among co-insurers.

C) Claim form: The policy holder will submit the claim form with the following information

(i) Name and address of the Insured.

(ii) Date of loss, time and place from where the fire started.

(iii) Cause of fire.

(iv) Details of the property damaged such as description, etc.

(v) Value at the time of fire, value of salvage and the amount of loss.

(vi) Details of other policies on the same property giving the name of the insurer, policy number and sum insured.

(vii) Fire Brigade report details.

(viii) F.I.R. at the nearest police station regarding third party liability, if any.

D) Settlement of claim: On the basis of the claim form and the survey report, decision is taken about the settlement or otherwise of the loss.

4.13 Health Insurance

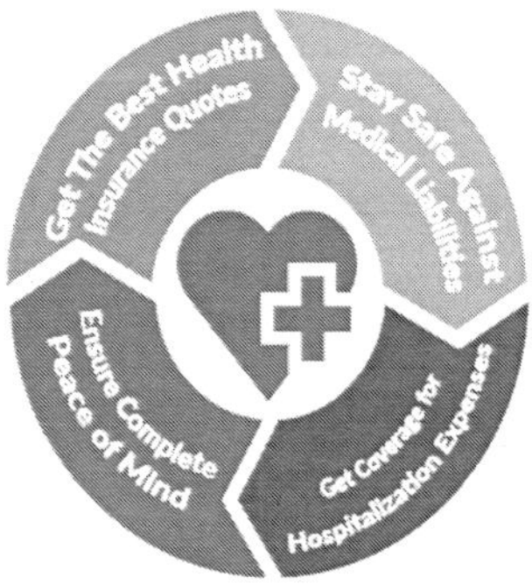

Meaning

Health insurance is a type of insurance coverage that pays for medical, surgical, and sometimes dental expenses incurred by the insured. Health insurance can reimburse the insured for expenses incurred from illness or injury, or pay the care provider directly.

Need for Health Insurance

Medicare or medical costs are rising year on year. As a matter of fact, inflation in medicare is higher than inflation in food and other articles. While inflation in food and clothing is in single digits, medicare costs usually escalate in double digits.For an individual who hasn't saved that much money, arranging for funds at the eleventh hour can be a task. This is particularly daunting for seniors, given that most ailments strike at an advanced age.

One way to provide for health-related / medical emergencies is by taking health insurance. Health insurance offers considerable flexibility in terms of disease / ailment coverage. For instance, certain health insurance plans cover as many as 30 critical illnesses and over 80 surgical procedures. The insurance plan disburses the payment towards surgery/illness regardless of actual medical expenses. The policy continues even after the benefit payment on selected illnesses. With health insurance, you are assured of a more secure future both health-wise and money-wise. This makes health insurance policies critical for individuals, especially if they are responsible for the financial well-being of the family.

4.13.1 Features of Health insurance

Get the Best Medical Care: The best health insurance plan certainly enables you to get your treatment done from the best doctors and hospitals in case you or any of your insured family members is hospitalized.

Transparent and Hassle-free Claims Settlement: The best mediclaim policy providers offer hassle-free claim settlement process with their health insurance plans. The best health insurance company also offers one of the fastest turnaround times in the industry by settling health insurance claims are under a few hours hour in case of cashless settlements. The best health insurance providers have one of the highest claims settlement ratios among other reputed health insurance providers in India.

Reasonably Priced Health Insurance Plans: You can enjoy maximum coverage at a price that is easy on your pocket when you choose to purchase the policy from the medical insurance providers

Cashless Settlement: Top health insurance companies are tied-up with a huge network of hospitals all over India. You can get cashless treatment at any of their registered network of cashless hospitals. All you'll have to do is just notify your insurer and the rest will be taken care of by them.

Peace of Mind: Well all are very much aware of the fact a medical emergencies doesn't come with a prior warning. It causes you to say goodbye to your financial savings. With the best health insurance policy you can be protected knowing that you and your family members will always be financially protected against any unforeseen medical or health care costs.

Health Benefits: The best mediclaim policy provides quick claim settlement through their user-friendly smartphone app.

Preventive Care: On your purchase of the best health insurance policy, you will be entitled avail free medical check-ups once every claim-free year.

Comprehensive coverage: The best mediclaim insurance providers in India lets you freely choose from a wide range of affordable health insurance policies to cover you and your family against various critical illnesses, accidents and medical expenses. Furthermore, the best health insurers enable you to go for added top-up plans to avail extra coverage in exchanged of extra premium.

Ease of Transaction: The top health insurance companies lets their customers buy or renew their policy online. You can simply visit the official website of your health insurer and secure your health in just a few clicks online.

24x7 On-Call Customer Service: The best health insurance providers will always be on your service through an in-house Health Administration Team to make sure that their policyholders get a swift and seamless claims settlement experience.

4.13.2 Health insurance Schemes

Rashtriya Swasthya Bima Yojana (RSBY): This scheme of Government of India is especially launched to offer the health insurance benefits to the families that are below property line. This plan offers financial protection for the unorganized workers. Ministry of Labor and Employment under the Central Government has launched this scheme.

Pradhan Matri Suraksha Bima Yojana: This Government scheme is beneficial for those families that belong to economically underprivileged sections of the Indian society. This scheme financially securing those families with a sum insured of up to Rs. 2 lakhs. It is specially designed to financially protect families and individuals against death, and partial and total disability.

Aam Aadmi Bima Yojana: The scheme was launched in 2013. This government scheme has been tailor-made for addressing the 48 occupational groups or rural areas with landless households. The amalgamation of Aam Aadmi Bima Yojana (AABY) and Janashree Bima Yojana (JBY) has resulted in the newly formed scheme, named Aam Aadmi Bima Yojana. It offers medical insurance benefits to any one earning member of a family or the head of a family.

Ayushman Bharat: This scheme is specially launched by Government of India with the aim of offering benefits of up to Rs. 5 lakhs to 50 crore to the people who belong to underprivileged families throughout India. Ayushman Bharat is an ambitious scheme covering even pre-existing disease. This health insurance scheme can be availed at government as well as private hospitals. In other words, this plan offers comprehensive medical benefits to the deprived families

Universal Health Insurance Scheme (UHIS): It is an effective initiative of Indian Government and was launched in 2003. This scheme provides quality healthcare to Indian families that are below as well as above the poverty line, especially BPL families. Under this scheme compensation of Rs.30, 000/- is given to the insured and his or her family against medical expenses due to hospitalization. Even death of the earning member of the family due to any mishap is covered in this scheme.

Merits of Health Insurance

It's quite crystal clear by now that best mediclaim policy comes with myriads of benefits and special advantages that can't be replaced with anything. A policyholder can avail a number of advantages from their health insurance company. Though the benefits offered varies from one insurer to another insurer in India, there're some specific special features that can be by anyone opting for mediclaim policies online. Well, following the key benefits of having the best medical plan online.

Cashless Treatment Facility: Since our country India is emphasizing on digitization, you can almost see the adapted changes in the insurance sector as well. Cash is something that may not be available to everyone all the time and that is the reason why cashless treatments have taken a massive ground. In the event of hospitalization, if you are protected under a mediclaim cover that provide the facility of cashless treatment, you no longer have to worry about your medical bills payment because your insurance company will take care of the payment through cashless scheme on your behalf let you focus on the medical treatment only. Cashless treatment may prove out to be savior when you don't have arranged funds in the form of cash at the time of any medical emergency. All you have to do is choose a health insurance provider that offer cashless treatment facility to avail this benefit.

No Claim Bonus (NCB): No Claim Bonus (NCB) for medical policy stands for a specific amount of discount that you receive for not filing any claim during a policy term. This discount is applicable on your premium at the time of your mediclaim policy renewal. NCB triggers the health insurance policyholder to not file a claim during a policy period.

Co-payment: When you buy health insurance, you will come across to the term stated as co-pay. Co-pay stands for a pre specified amount that you have to pay before your insurance provider comes forward to settle down the rest of the medical bills when you file a claim. Your overall Sum Insured amount is not affected by co-payment.

Family Discounts: This discount is offered by health insurers companies in India for enrolling any family member or any person under a mediclaim policy. This is a form of reward offered by health insurers to existing policyholders for referring them to people.

24*7 Customer Support: To provide the customers the best assistance on anything related to their medical policy of coverage, the company provides round the clock customer care support.

Lifelong Renewability: Since it's important to pick the best medical cover that comes with the option of lifetime renewability, especially in the old age, health insurance companies in India has started offering health plans that can be renewed throughout lifetime of an insured person. Lifelong renewability is only applicable if there's no break in your health policy.

Free Health Check-Ups: Medical insurers provide free health check-up to encourage all its policyholder lead a healthy life. The free health check-up facility is provided only once in a while but that totally depends upon the type of plan you choose.

Online Buying & Renewal Option: Given that the entire world is being encapsulated into online, mediclaim policies also doesn't lag behind in terms of renewal or purchasing. Gone are the days when you had to wait and struggle a lot to avail the best mediclaim policy. Nowadays you can instantly buy or renew medical policy in an instant online. All the health insurers offer online renewal and buying facility for health insurance plans.

4.13.3 Types of Health Covers

Different Types of Health Covers in India

Individual Health Insurance Plan: This is one of the best mediclaim policies that everyone is more or less familiar with in India. Like the name suggests, Individual medical plans are exclusively designed for the health protection of an individual person against various critical illness under one Sum Insured. Though family members can be included under the best Individual medical policy but you'll have to choose a different Sum Insured for each family member you want to insure. The premium you'll pay for this medical policy is, in general, directly proportional to the Sum Insured.

Family Floater Plan: Family Floater Mediclaim policy offer an extensive medical coverage against various illnesses and diseases to all you family members under the single Sum Insured. This medical policy can cover your parents, spouse and dependent children. The premium of family floater cover is comparatively lower than the individual mediclaim policies taken by each family member. Family floater policy is significant given that it covers each of the family members and also provides a fixed Sum Insured for all insured members for single or multiple claims raised during the policy term.

Senior Citizen Health Insurance Plans: Like the name suggests, this specific medical cover is particularly designed for the senior citizens in India. As mandated by IRDAI, every insurance company must include people up to 65 years of age under senior citizen mediclaim plan.

Critical Illness Plans: Again one of the best mediclaim policies, critical illness plan is designed to provide medical coverage to insured persons against various critical illnesses specified under the policy. Given that the medication cost of such critical illness like cancer, paralysis, heart attack, kidney failure etc are expensive, the critical illness policy provides financial assistance in case the insured person is diagnosed with one of multiple critical illnesses listed under the policy.

Maternity Policy: Almost all the best health insurers in India offer maternity insurance policy nowadays. This mediclaim cover covers the costs incurred from child delivery, Pre & Post Natal care, and even sometimes covers the vaccination costs of the new born babies. To break it down in one sentence, maternity policy takes care of all your maternity expenditures. However, you should note that the features and benefits of this particular mediclaim policy may vary from one insurer to another.

Unit Linked Health Plan (ULHP): Unit Linked Health Plan (ULH) is a recently introduced medical plan in India that is similar to Unit Linked Insurance Plan (ULIP). ULHP is basically a grouping of a mediclaim plans and a market-linked investment plan. In spite of providing protection on health, Unit Linked Health Plan contributes in the construction of a structure that could be utilized to meet the expenses that are not covered by medical covers

Health Insurance Claim Settlement Procedure

Though most people are concerned about how TPAs work, still many don't know how health insurance claims are settled. The best medical company in India will settle your health claims as soon as possible. The time of health claim settlement may vary. For the claim on your mediclaim policy, the insured must approach the TPA for all formalities and verification process. It takes generally two days to settle claims for TPAs. Here's how health insurance claims are settled.

Cashless

Cashless treatment can be availed only through the network hospital of your best health insurance company in India. You must intimate the TPA prior to pre-planned hospitalization, or within a specific time duration in case of an emergency. The hospital's insurance desk will assist you with all the paperwork. The TPA needs to approve the mediclaim amount and thereafter the insurance company will settle the bills with the hospital except some excluded costs that have to be settled from the pocket of the patient party directly.

Reimbursement

Reimbursement facility can be availed both at networked and non-networked hospitals by the patients. With this facility, you will have to settle your mediclaim bills directly with the hospital after treatment. Thereafter you can file health insurance claim reimbursement of the expenditures from the TPA by providing the relevant receipts and bills.

4.13.4 Health insurance companies In India

Health Insurance Companies

Star Health and Allied Insurance:

A dedicated health insurance company with a wide network of hospitals.

Care Health Insurance:

Offers a range of comprehensive health insurance plans.

Niva Bupa Health Insurance:

Provides various health insurance solutions for individuals and families.

Aditya Birla Health Insurance:

Known for its health and wellness-focused plans.

ManipalCigna Health Insurance:

A joint venture offering diverse health insurance products.

General Insurance Companies Offering Health Insurance

HDFC ERGO General Insurance:

Provides a wide array of health insurance plans as part of its general insurance portfolio.

ICICI Lombard General Insurance:

Offers various health insurance products alongside its other general insurance offerings.

Bajaj Allianz General Insurance:

Provides comprehensive health insurance plans.

Tata AIG General Insurance:

Offers a variety of health insurance products.

SBI General Insurance:

Has a growing health insurance portfolio.

Go Digit General Insurance:

Offers digitally focused health insurance products.

Important Considerations:

When choosing a health insurance provider, consider factors like:

- Claim settlement ratio.
- Network of hospitals.
- Coverage and benefits.
- Customer service.

Chapter - 5

Marine Insurance

Meaning

Marine insurance covers the loss or damage of ships, cargo, terminals, and any transport by which the property is transferred, acquired, or held between the points of origin and the final destination. When goods are transported by mail or courier, shipping insurance is used instead.

5.1 Functions of Marine Insurance

- The basic requirement of marine insurance is to provide you with peace of mind while conducting your business. Let us understand how it works:
- Evaluate and analyse your requirement regarding the risks involved and the loss that you would incur in case of any eventuality
- After preparing your list, check and compare the companies and policies to understand where you would get the best deal
- After zeroing in on the plan, get the documents in place for purchasing the policy
- In case of any untoward incident for which you would need a claim, immediately inform the insurance provider
- Submit the duly filled in claim form along with the required documents, proofs and certificates
- In case the claim is considered fit, you would get the claim, else it will be rejected

5.1.2 Types of Marine Insurance

There are four types of Marine Insurance

Hull Insurance - Covers the insurance of the vessel and its equipment i.e. furniture and fittings, machinery, tools, fuel, etc. It is affected generally by the owner of the ship.

Cargo Insurance - Includes the cargo or goods contained in the ship and the personal belongings of the crew and passengers.

Freight Insurance - Provides protection against the loss of freight. In many cases, the owner of goods is bound to pay freight, under the terms of the contract, only when the goods are safely delivered at the port of destination. If the ship is lost on the way or the cargo is damaged or stolen, the shipping company loses the freight. Freight insurance is taken to guard against such risk.

Liability Insurance - Is one in which the insurer undertakes to indemnify against the loss which the insured may suffer on account of liability to a third party caused by collision of the ship and other similar hazards. In a contract of marine insurance, the insured must have insurable interest in the subject matter insured at the time of the loss. Insurable interest is not required to be present at the time of taking the policy.

Under marine insurance, the following persons are deemed to have insurable interest The owner of the ship has an insurable interest in the ship.

The owner of the cargo has insurable interest in the cargo.

- A creditor who has advanced money on the security of the ship or cargo has insurable interest to the extent of his loan.
- The master and crew of the ship have insurable interest in respect of their wages.
- If the subject matter of insurance is mortgaged, the mortgagor has insurable interest in the full value thereof, and the mortgagee has insurable interest in respect of any sum due to him.
- A trustee holding any property in trust has insurable interest in such property.
- In case of advance freight the person advancing the freight has an insurable interest in so far as such freight is repayable in case of loss.
- The insured has an insurable interest in the charges of any insurance policy which he may take.

5.1.3 Types of Marine Insurance Policies

1. Voyage Policy - Is a policy in which the subject matter is insured for a particular voyage irrespective of the time involved in it. In this case the risk attaches only when the ship starts on the voyage.

Time Policy -Is a policy in which the subject matter is insured for a definite period of time. The ship may pursue any course it likes; the policy would cover all the risks from perils of the sea for the stated period of time. A time policy cannot be for a period exceeding one year, but it may contain a 'continuation clause'. The 'continuation clause' means that if the voyage is not completed within the specified period, the risk shall be covered until the voyage is completed, or till the arrival of the ship at the port of call.

2. Mixed Policy - Is a combination of voyage and time policies and covers the risk during particular voyage for a specified period of time.

3. Valued Policy - Is a policy in which the value of the subject matter insured is agreed upon between the insurer and the insured and it is specified in the policy itself.

4. Open or Un-valued Policy - Is the policy in which the value of the subject matter insured is not specified. Subject to the limit of the sum assured, it leaves the value of the loss to be subsequently ascertained.

5. Floating or Declaration Policy - Is a policy which only mentions the amount for which the insurance is taken out and leaves the name of the ship(s) and other particulars to be defined by subsequent declarations. Such policies are very useful to merchants who regularly despatch goods through ships.

5.1.4 Procedure for effective marine insurance

Generally, the following steps are to be adopted while taking out a marine insurance policy:

1. Selection of the Company
2. Selection of Agent or Broker
3. Marine Declaration Form
4. Assessment of the Risk
5. Payment of premium
6. Issue of Cover Note
7. Issue of Policy

Advantages of Marine Insurance

While conducting business involving cargo and sea ways, it makes sense to opt for a marine insurance. Some of the advantages of purchasing this insurance are:

- The insurance provides financial stability to the business
- It helps manage the risks and conduct business without much worries
- It compensates for any financial loss that one faces during the transit of goods

Principles of Marine Insurance

Basic Principles of Marine Insurance: The basic principles which govern the insurance are

- Utmost good faith
- Insurable interest
- Indemnity
- Subrogation
- Proximate cause
- Contribution
- Abandonment

5.1.4 Importance of marine insurance

Before purchasing a marine policy, you should always check the companies and policies before finalizing the one that suits you. Let us look at certain points to be kept in mind:

- As far as cargo insurance is concerned, the sum insured is calculated on the basis of cost, insurance and freight (CIF) value mentioned in the invoices. The insurance company generally agrees to the sum insured up to 10% to 15% higher value than total CIF value mentioned in the invoice.
- For insurance related to ship-owners, the sum insured is finalized after complex calculations. The factors like the route of the ship, the number of ships in the fleet, past claim history of the shipping line, safety and precautions arranged at various transit points, etc. are taken into consideration. Still, there are grey areas, which ship owners should carefully handle for comprehensive coverage of the ship, cargo and people inside the ship.

- The mode of transport for your cargo can be rail, road, water, air or a combination of more than two modes. Under such uncertainty, it is advisable to make sure that your marine policy assumes global coverage and you will get worldwide assistance for survey and settlement of your claim.

5.1.5 Claim Process

After purchasing the marine insurance, in case there arises a situation when you need to make a claim under the policy, you can follow the below mentioned steps

- In case of loss or damage to the cargo or the ship, you need to immediately inform the insurance provider
- A surveyor will assess the damage or loss mentioned
- All the proofs and witnesses need to be submitted along with the duly filled in claim form
- For a missing package, the insured must lodge file a monetary claim with the insurance provider and get an acknowledgement for it
- If the provider finds the case fit, it would approve the claim, else it would reject it
- In case you are not satisfied with the case, you can approach the court of law

Documents Required for Claim Process

To make the claims under marine insurance and be able to reap the benefits, the correct documents should be submitted. In case of any lapse, there is a chance of the risk being rejected. Some of the documents are:

- Duly filled in claim form
- Original insurance certificate with the policy number
- Copy of Billing Lading
- Survey report or missing certificate
- Original invoice, packing list, shipping specification
- Copies of correspondence exchanged

Exclusions

Marine insurance has various kinds of coverage for the benefit of all. However, the policy does not cover certain situations, also called exclusions. Some of these cases are:

- Wilful, planned or intentional misconduct
- Strike, rioting, war
- Poor packaging quality of the cargo
- Delays
- General leakage or wear and tear of the cargo
- Financial distress or insolvency of the shipping line
- Removal of wreck

5.1.6 Companies Offering Marine Insurance in India

Looking at the fact that India is surrounded by water from three sides, shipping is an important sector. A big volume of cargo is managed at these ports, making this insurance an important requirement. Some of the companies providing marine insurance in India are:

- All major banks and financial institutions
- HDFC Ergo
- TATA AIG
- United India Insurance Company
- Royal Sundaram
- New India Assurance Company Limited
- Bharti AXA

5.2 Motor Insurance

Meaning

Motor insurance is the insurance policy for vehicles. It could include Car Insurance and Two-Wheeler Insurance. Vehicles that are used for commercial purposes, like buses and trucks, are covered by Commercial Vehicle Insurance. ... It is compulsory to buy auto insurance when you purchase a vehicle.

5.2.1 Types of Motor Insurance

Motor insurance can be availed in three Types

1. Private Car Insurance
2. Commercial Vehicle Insurance
3. Two Wheeler Insurance

1. Private Car Insurance - Private Car Insurance should be first thing to be taken after purchasing a Car. A financial safeguard for a large variety of situations, Private Car Insurance is one of the most important purchases to make. Whether it is a natural disaster such as an earthquake or flood; or somebody damages or steals the car, a Car Insurance takes care of it all. With compulsory factors such as third-party liability, one can ensure that any damage occurred to another person's life or property by his vehicle will be covered in a claim. You can also opt for the Motor Insurance Add-on plans, such as zero depreciation, engine & gear box protector, emergency assistance, cost of consumables etc. which enhances your coverage for better protection, in addition to your standard motor insurance policy.

2. Commercial Vehicle Insurance - To keep the business going, it is imperative for business owners to have the vehicles owned by them insured. General insurance providers offer packaged commercial vehicle insurance policies which protect businesses from potential financial loss to the vehicle arising out of accidental loss or damage, the legal liability towards third-parties for bodily injury, death or property damage on account of any accident involving the vehicle. Insurance is available on commercial vehicles like trucks, Private as well as Public Carriers, Trailers, Taxis, 3-wheeler Autos, Buses, Miscellaneous and Special Types of vehicles – Agricultural Mobile Rig,

Shovels, Grabs, Tractor, and Excavator etc.

Basic Motor Insurance coverage includes:

- Loss or damage by accident, fire, lightning, self-ignition, external explosion, burglary, housebreaking or theft, malicious act.
- Liability for third party injury/death, third party property and liability to paid driver On payment of appropriate additional premium, loss/damage to electrical/electronic accessories can be covered.

3. Two Wheeler Insurance: As soon as you purchase a two wheeler, getting two wheeler insurance is a mandatory requirement as per the Motor Vehicles Act 1988 and Motor Vehicle Amendment Act 2019. It provides coverage for from any financial loss to the vehicle due to accidental loss or damage, the legal liability towards third-parties in event of bodily injury, death or property damage. It also offers coverage in event of damage due to natural calamities or manmade events.

Coverage of Motor Insurance

Own Damage to your vehicle - The policy covers you against any loss or damage caused to your car or it's accessories due to natural and manmade calamities as defined in the scope of coverage

(i) Personal Accident Cover - The motor insurance provides you compulsory personal accident cover for individual owners of the vehicle, the personal accident cover is up to Rs. 2 lacs. You can also opt for a personal accident cover for passengers. Rs.2 Lac is the maximum coverage that can be offered.

Third Party legal liability - The policy covers the vehicle owner's legal liability to pay compensation for:

- Death or bodily injury to a third party person
- Damage to third party property

Liability is covered for an unlimited amount in respect of death or injury and damage to third party property for Rs.7.5 laks under Commercial vehicle and private and Rs. 1 lacs for Scooters / Motor Cycles.

5.2.2 Claim Process

Formalities for a motor insurance claim

A claim under a motor insurance policy could be

For personal injury or property damage related to someone else. This person is called a third party in this context) or

For damage to your own, insured, vehicle. This is called an own damage claim and you are eligible for this if you are holding what is known as a package or a comprehensive policy.

Third Party Claim

In a third party claim, where your vehicle is involved, it is important to ensure that the accident is reported immediately to the police as well as to the insurance company.

On the other hand, if you are a victim, that is, if somebody else's vehicle was involved, you must obtain the insurance details of that vehicle and make intimation to the insurer of that vehicle.

Own Damage Claim

In the event of an own damage claim, that is, where your own vehicle is damaged due to an accident, you must immediately inform insurance company and police, wherever required, to enable them to depute a surveyor to assess the loss.

Do not attempt to move the vehicle from the accident spot without the permission of police and the insurance company.

Once you receive permission for removal of the vehicle and for repairs, you can do so.

If your policy provides for cashless service, which means you do not have to pay out of your pocket for covered damages, the insurance company will pay the workshop directly.

In either of these situations, you must intimate the insurance company immediately.

Theft Claim

If your vehicle is stolen, you must inform the police and the insurance company immediately. In addition you must keep the transport department also informed.

As soon as you receive the policy document, read about the procedures and documentation requirements for claims rather than wait for a claim to arise.

If you have to make a claim, ensure that you collect all the required documents and submit them along with the requisite claim form duly filled in, to the insurance company.

There may be certain specific documentation requirements for specific types of claims. For instance in respect of a theft claim, there is a special requirement that you should surrender the vehicle keys to the insurance company.

5.3 Rural Insurance

Meaning

Rural insurance ensures that families living in rural areas have a safe and secure future so that they can lead a happy life. The insurance helps them to cover risks related to various aspects of their life. Rural Insurance policies come with the affordable premium rates and faster claim process

Rural insurance includes a wide range of plans to cover various sections. Some of them are

Plans	Definition
Motor Insurance	Comprehensive coverage for agricultural vehicles like tractors, cars, scooters, trailers and motorcycles
Property Insurance	Covers home, shops, retail outlets, schools and agricultural equipment
Accident Insurance	Covers accidental death, partial or total disability of the insured
Livestock Insurance	Insurance coverage for cattle against death or disability
Health Insurance	Personal accident insurance and Mediclaim for the insured
Poultry Insurance	Covers broilers and parent stock of chicken

Rural insurance is associated with the lifestyle risks of people residing in villages. This insurance policy includes:

- Hut insurance
- Poultry insurance
- Cycle rickshaw policy
- Sericulture insurance
- Honey bee insurance
- Failed- well insurance
- Sheep and goat insurance
- Lift irrigation insurance

- Farmers' package insurance
- Agricultural pump-set policy
- Animal-driven cart insurance
- Gramin personal accident insurance
- Aqua-culture (prawn/ shrimp) insurance
- Horticulture/ plantation insurance scheme
- Animals included in rural insurance are elephants, rabbits, pigs, birds, zoo and circus animals

5.3.1 Functions of Rural Insurance

Analyze your requirement and the loss associated with your assets so that you know which type of insurance to opt for

- The analysis will also help in deciding the premium amount
- Check and compare various insurance companies and plans to pick up the best one for you
- The insurer checks whether the applicant resides in the rural area
- The premium is mutually agreed between the insurer and the insured after going through the property/ livestock details
- When a risk occurs, the insured immediately informs the bank/insurer company about the mishap
- Evidence of the event, duly filled claim form and FIR Report (if needed) are submitted by the insured
- The claim is verified by bank officials. If authentic, the claim is settled, else it is rejected

5.3.2 Eligibility Criteria for Rural Insurance

According to the Insurance Regulatory and Development Authority of India (IRDA), rural sector which is eligible for this insurance has to fulfil the following categories:

- Has a population less than 5,000 people
- Density of population is not more than 400 per square kilometre
- Minimum 75% of male population must be engaged in farming activities

Claim Process

After the eventuality, inform the insurance company as soon as possible

Provide the duly filled in claim form along with the required documents

- Submit the proofs and certificates
- After an assessment, if the provider finds it fit, your claim will be accepted and you will receive your compensation, else it will be rejected
- If you are not satisfied with the decision, you can approach the court of law some of the documents required to be submitted to the insurance company for making claims are:
- Duly filled in claim form
- Photocopy of insurance policy
- FIR report in case of accidents/ vandalism
- Death certificate (in case of death of the insured)
- Evidence of equipment damage (in case of property insurance) Ear

Time taken to settle claims

Rural insurance claim is processed and settled within 30 days of submitting the supporting documents. If further investigation is needed, the insurance company can take maximum of 3 months.

5.3.3 Exclusions

Though rural insurance has different sets of exclusions, which are

Plans	Exclusions
Cattle Insurance	• Death/ disability caused by neglect, overloading or treatment by unskilled people • Intentional slaughter without permission of government authorities • Theft/clandestine sale

Poultry Insurance	• Death caused by overcrowding • Transit by any transport • Theft/clandestine sale • Intentional slaughter without the • permission of government authority
Motor Insurance	• Loss/damage from theft • Vehicle confiscated/destroyed by government body
Property Insurance	• Cost of dismantling to and from transport to workshop • Faults existing at the time of commencement of the policy • Damage for which the supplier/ manufacturer is responsible

Advantages of Rural Insurance

It is important to spread awareness about various types of rural insurance so that people residing in rural areas get to benefit from schemes meant for them. Some of the benefits of purchasing rural insurance are:

- Easy to understand plans
- People have to pay low premium which can be affordable
- The plan can compensate for monetary losses covered under the plan
- The plan can help people in rural areas become independent

Companies Offering Rural Insurance in India

- TATA AIG
- Aviva India

- Cholamandalam
- Oriental Insurance
- IFFCO Tokio

5.4 Crop Insurance

5.4.1 Introduction

Every year, in one part of India or the other food crops are affected by natural calamities, "Crop yield instability is the normal condition and agriculture continues still to be which the farmer's fortunes are exposed, is practically the same as before. In fact, good years and bad years, wet weather and drought or floods and frost, low yields and bumper crops are to be expected in mixed succession. The total loss due to natural calamities (like flood, drought and plant diseases) is estimated as high as Rs. 1,000 crores every year. The man behind the plough has to be assured that he will be compensated for such loss in crops. Otherwise, he cannot be drawn into the campaign to increase productivity of land under his plough,"

Definiton

In the words of Shri S. K. Patil, "Crop insurance is the Mangna Charta of the Indian agriculturists. It will mitigate rural poverty and will change the psychology of the Indian farmer in a radical manner."

5.4.2 Reasons for the Crop Insurance

(1) In our country Nature has always been moody. "She is unpredictably generous to one state and disconcertingly bad-tempered to another. This fickleness of weather conditions in different parts of the country upsets the whole agricultural economy, and makes one part bountiful, while the other starves."

(2) Besides droughts and floods, locusts, plant diseases have always been a serious enemy to our agriculture by destroying standing crops and thereby reducing farmers' income.

(3) Majority of the holdings are tiny, form which the farmers get marginal surplus in good years and incur heavy deficits in the bad ones.

(4) Farming is more hazardous than any other enterprise. The weather can make all the differencc between success and failure. Consequently, many farmers, particularly the small ones, feel shy of adopting new techniques.

The fear of loss is so overwhelming that even when convinced of the gain accruing from the application of science and technology, they prefer to go along the traditional track of low productivity. Once freed from fear by crop insurance they can quicken the pace to high productivity.

The Fourth Plan observed, "Severe distress is caused to the farmers by crop failure resulting from drought, floods and other natural calamities. This risk is likely to get accentuated under conditions of large investments in fertilizers, pesticides, improved seeds and other inputs which are proposed to be used on a large scale during the Fourth Plan. One of the important means of alleviating distress arising out from natural calamities could be the organisation of crop insurance."

5.4.3 Nature of Crop Insurance

Crop insurance makes up the loss or damage to growing crops resulting from a variety of causes such as hail or drought frost, flood and disease. The cultivators pay a premium and protection is given to them on the same basis as in other insurance. When the production from an insured acreage falls below the insured coverage, the tiller is entitled to an indemnity.

Coverage and premium rates are settled on the basis of productivity and susceptibility to risk of the lands under cultivation in the same, area. Besides an all-risk crop insurance, there are three other main types of insurance to cover the risk from fire, hail and flood.

5.4.4 Scenario of Crop Insurance in India:

The idea of crop insurance in India was mooted about 3 decades ago, when a Sub-Committee on "Land Policy, Agricultural Labour and Insurance," inter alia, had recommended a national scheme of cattle and' crop insurance with agriculturist, the village or the district and the nation collectively contributing to its successful operation.

The first concrete step towards introduction of the insurance scheme was taken by the Govt. in 1948, when a special officer Dr. G.S. Priolker was appointed to investigate a systematic and scientific a basis for formulating an experimental pilot scheme.

Dr. Priolker in his Report, 1949, recommended a pilot scheme covering 4 crops, (rice, wheat, cotton and sugarcane). Tamil Nadu (rice and cotton), Maharashtra and Gujarat (cotton), M. P. (cotton, wheat and rice) and U.P. (wheat, rice and sugarcane) were suggested for experimentation.

5.4.5 Merits of Crop Insurance

The advantages of crop insurance are recognized on all hands:

(i) It provides protection to farmers against losses caused by crop failure and thereby ensures stability in farm income,

(ii) It also strengthens the position of co-operatives and other institutions that finance, agriculture to the extent it enables the farmer members to repay their loans in years of crop failure,

(iii) By protecting the economic interest of the farmers against possible risk or loss, it accelerates adoption of new agricultural practices,

(iv) It minimizes the problem of rural indebtedness, which is traceable to the frequent failure of crops,

(v) It also reduces, to some extent, government expenditure incurred on relief measures extended to meet the havoc caused by natural calamities,

(vi) It may act as anti-inflationary measure, by locking up part of the resources in rural areas.

Speaking of the many advantages flowing from the crop insurance, an official of the U.S. Federal Crop Insurance Corporation said that it is "fundamentally for the purpose of creating catastrophic insurance and is intended to insure a minimum return to the farmer which enables him to stay in business in case of severe loss. The justification for the Government insurance is not alone the need of protection, of the individual farmer and his continued income and buying power. This affects vitally like labour, industry, trade, banking and the entire community of which the farmer is a part."

5.4.6 The financial responsibility of the State Governments

(a) Entire expenses of administration,

(b) Direct subsidy, and

(c) Operating deficits.

The scheme was examined by an expert committee, which suggested the introduction of the scheme at 12 centres. In 1952 the four States of Maharashtra and Gujarat, Uttar Pradesh, Tamil Nadu and M. P. were asked whether they would be able to implement the scheme by sharing 50% cost on State level organization.

While M.P. was willing to try the scheme if the entire cost were borne by the Centre, the other States were not willing to undertake it. The scheme was later examined by the FAO Working Committee meeting at Bangkok in 1956. Experts in insurance and agriculture also considered it suitable for implementation. On account of financial stringencies, however, the Government of India decided to defer the introduction of the scheme

5.4.7 Punjab Experience:

In 1961 Punjab Government decided to implement a modified version of the pilot scheme in certain selected areas of Punjab. According to the scheme, two of the four principal crops, viz., wheat, gram, cotton and sugarcane, are to be insured. It is compulsory, that is to say, all the cultivators who grow any two of the insured crops will have to participate in the scheme. All natural hazards are covered under the scheme. For the purpose of indemnities and premium rates a block is divided into a number of areas homogeneous regarding soil, cultivation practices and production risks. Indemnities and premium rates are to be fixed separately for each crop and each homogeneous area.

Crop failures are to' be assessed objectively and if the indemnities become payable in respect of an insured crop, every cultivator growing that crop in the area will get indemnities whether or not he suffered loss of yield in respect of that crop. Indemnities are payable when the seasonal yield calls below 75% of the normal yield. The maximum indemnity payable in case of total loss of crop will be 50% of the normal yield. The premium rates for a crop in a given area will be such that the premia collected over a number of years balance the indemnities payable over that period. Seasonal yields for the determination of indemnities will be fixed by an objective method of crop-cutting experiments by the field staff provided under the scheme. The administrative cost of the scheme will be shouldered by the Govt. The scheme is to be administered by a Crop Insurance Board which will include agricultural exports and insurance experts as members.

The Punjab scheme has several limitations. The key principle of insurance requires that indemnity will correspond with the loss but the Punjab farmer, under this pilot scheme is assured of indemnity irrespective of his having suffered an actual loss or not Premium rates have been fixed in, such a way that, collected over a number of years, the amount will balance the indemnities payable over the period. If his presupposes that the farmer will have to shoulder the losses due to natural calamities, This might make the farmers feel that they are bearing a new tax burden, a feeling that should be avoided. The administrative cost which is to be shared by the Central and the State Govts, on a 50: 50 basis will be about Rs. 7 lakhs per year, which comes to about 17.5% of the premia collected. The cost seems to be on the very high side. Nevertheless in the Third Plan, a sum of Rs. 40 lakhs was allotted for the purpose. The programme could be put into operation because of the constitutional hitch insurance being a central 'subject, a State Govt. cannot run even a pilot scheme without an enabling legislation by the Parliament. Therefore, in July, 1967, a Bill known as a Crop Insurance Bill was drafted and the pilot scheme for the introduction of compulsory crop scheme was forwarded to the State Governments for support. Punjab has collected requisite data in selected area. The scheme covers wheat, gram, cotton and sugarcane, and will be extended to cover other crops and other areas in the State. During the Fourth Plan, crop insurance scheme was extended to other States. Legislation was envisaged for the introduction of crop insurance on a compulsory basis by the States. To finance the scheme, a Crop Insurance Fund of about Rs. 100 crores has been contemplated. The main difficulty in introducing crop insurance scheme is the non-availability of essential data like loss rates in different year, heavy financial resources, bad luck of experienced and trained personnel.

But these difficulties are not insurmoun table.

There are certain areas in some States where pilot schemes can be introduced. For example, we may perhaps suggest 2 or 3 districts in Punjab, Tamil Nadu, Maharashtra and Gujarat for selected crops. More particularly, crop insurance can be experimented within those areas where the crop loan system has been introduced and met with a success.

5.5 Natural Calamities

5.5.1 Introduction

A natural disaster is the effect of a natural hazard - (e.g. flood, tornado, hurricane, volcanic eruption, earthquake, or landslide) that affects the environment, and leads to financial, environmental and/or human losses. The World is always changing.

5.5.2 Causes of Natural calamities

A natural disaster is a major bad event caused by the natural processes of the Earth. Examples include floods, hurricanes, tornadoes, volcanic eruptions, earthquakes, tsunamis and other geologic processes. A natural disaster causes loss of life or property damage, and leaves some economic damage afterwards.

5.5.3 Types of Natural calamities

Different types of natural disasters include floods, earthquakes, hurricanes, volcanic eruptions and many more. There are varying estimates that peg the number of natural disasters per year across the world in the range of 500-1000.

5.6 Theft Insurance

What's considered theft in insurance?

Insurance protects you from sudden, unexpected things that may happen to you (or that you may accidentally do to others). Theft fits the bill... as long as you're not the thief.

What's cool about this named peril (if we can say perils are cool?!) is that your insurer will cover your stuff both at home and anywhere else, even abroad! So if your earrings are stolen from your hotel safe while you're out to dinner, or someone swipes your purse when you're out sightseeing, you're covered!

Does renters / homeowners insurance cover theft?

Yes!

As we mentioned above, theft is a named peril (which also include other bad things that may happen to your stuff because of fire, vandalism, freezing, and more). Renters insurance always covers theft – and homeowners insurance covers theft, too. That said, like most parts of your insurance policy, there are a few exceptions you should note.

Theft isn't covered if

You're the one who stole something

It happened somewhere you rent/own that's under construction

It happened at your place when someone's renting it out

While the first is pretty obvious, the second two are less so.

Insurance is there to protect you from sudden, accidental events that you couldn't have prevented on your own – essentially unforeseeable risks. Places that are under construction or rented out to others carry a much higher risk of something happening to your stuff, and are therefore excluded from your coverage.

Read: that super fancy watch you left in your room while renting out your place that was stolen? Not covered by your insurance company.

When theft is covered... and when it isn't

Now let's dig into some practical examples of when theft would and wouldn't be covered by your insurance company:

Example 1: Burglarized apartment

Let's say you go out for a movie with a friend, and come home to find that a burglar broke into your place and stole your TV, computer, sound system, a bunch of expensive jewelry, and your friend's backpack which had a laptop and headphones inside. Ouch.

Would you be covered? Yes, mostly.

First off, your and your friend's stuff would be covered, provided they don't have a policy of their own. Just make sure you can provide a full inventory of what was stolen, make and

model, receipts, and pictures if possible. The more info you can get, the easier it will be for your claims adjuster and insurance company to process your claim.

The only tricky thing in this scenario is the expensive jewelry.

Most companies provide around $1,500 of insurance coverage for jewelry under your base insurance policy. If your jewelry was worth more than that, you'll need to have something called an endorsement to add on extra coverage in order for it to be protected in scenarios like this. Otherwise, if your jewelry was worth more than $1,500 and it wasn't properly insured, you may be in a bit of a pickle.

Now, for another example.

Example 2: House swap theft

Let's say you did a house swap with a couple you found on Facebook, and came back to find that they stole a bunch of stuff including cash, jewelry, TVs, and watches.

Unfortunately, since you willingly let others stay in your home, you're actually on the hook for this.

To sum it all up, don't let strangers into your home and always make sure you have enough coverage for your stuff!

References

1. Hull, J. C. (2018). *Risk management and financial institutions.* John Wiley & Sons.
2. Rao, K. S. (2020). The development of the insurance industry in India. *Indian Journal of Finance, 12*(4), 67-82.
3. "Insurance." (2024). Britannica Academic. Retrieved from https://www.britannica.com/topic/insurance
4. Rejda, G. E. (2015). *Principles of risk management and insurance.* Pearson.
5. Mishra, M. (2018). *Insurance: Principles and practice.* Excel Books.
6. The Insurance Act, 1938. (1938). Government of India.
7. Life Insurance Corporation Act, 1956. (1956). Government of India.
8. Insurance Regulatory and Development Authority Act, 1999. (1999). Government of India.